The Heart Healing Journey

Awaken, Heal and Transform Your Life

MARK DEJESUS

All rights reserved. This book may not be copied or reprinted for commercial gain or profit. The use of short quotations or occasional page copying for personal or group study is permitted and encouraged.

Unless otherwise indicated, all Scripture quotations are taken from the New King James Version of the Bible. Copyright © 1982 by Thomas Nelson, Inc. Used by permission. All rights reserved.

Please note the writing style in this book chooses to capitalize certain pronouns in Scripture that refer to God the Father, the Son, and the Holy Spirit, and may differ from other publishing styles. Web Sites that are referenced were up to date at the time of publishing and are not endorsed unless specifically stated so in the writing.

The Heart Healing Journey: *Awaken, Heal and Transform Your Life*
By Mark DeJesus

MarkDeJesus.com   TurningHeartsMinistries.org
© 2019 – Mark DeJesus & Turning Hearts Ministries
Published by: Turning Hearts Ministries International

ISBN: 9781080422814

Cover Design by: zenefashions and 99designs.
This cover has been designed using resources from https://www.freepik.com/free-photos-vectors/background
background photo created by whatwolf
https://www.freepik.com/free-photos-vectors/people
people photo created by jcomp

Editorial Assistance Provided by: Melissa DeJesus

Additional Editorial Assistance Provided by: Chris Molitor

All rights reserved.

CONTENTS

THE HEART HEALING JOURNEY I
CONTENTS III
DEDICATION I
DISCLAIMER 1
INTRODUCTION 3
01: TENDING TO YOUR GARDEN 7
02: HOW'S YOUR HEART? 15
03: THE FOUNDATION IS CRACKED 25
04: RECOVERING YOUR FOOTING 35
05: CULTIVATING HEART AWARENESS 43
06: WAKING UP TO YOUR BROKENNESS 51
07: WHAT IS A BROKEN HEART? 59
08: KNOWING WHAT YOU NEED 69
09: AWAKENED TO THE BATTLE 79
10: THE FOUR DOORWAYS (PART 1) 88
11: THE FOUR DOORWAYS (PART 2) 95
12: THE WOUNDS WE ALL CARRY 101
13: THE POWER OF SELF-ACCEPTANCE 111
14: YOUR NEED FOR PATIENCE 119
15: WHAT DOES LOVE SAY? 125
16: KICKING OUT THE INNER PHARISEE 135
17: PERMISSION TO FEEL 144
18: RECEIVING THE SIGNALS FROM EMOTIONAL PAIN 153
19: STUCK IN YOUR HEAD 161
20: LEARNING TO GRIEVE 167

21: HEALING MEMORIES 175
22: HEALING FROM TRAUMA 183
23: RECEIVING GOD'S GUIDANCE 193
24: DECISIONS...DECISIONS 203
25: RESTORING JOY 209
26: LIVING POWERFULLY WITH A SENSITIVE HEART 219
27: FINDING SAFE RELATIONSHIPS 227
28: TURNING THE TABLES ON YOUR PAIN 237

Dedication

To the remnant of people who have decided to live as overcomers, with hearts awakened, positioned for healing, this book is dedicated to you. It's been an honor to work behind the scenes with people from all kinds of backgrounds and walks of life. May your healing journey impact the masses and generations to come.

Disclaimer

The content published is for informational purposes. The content included in this book is not intended to be a substitute for professional advice, diagnosis, or treatment. Always seek the advice of your mental health professional or other qualified health provider with any questions you may have regarding your condition. Never disregard professional advice or delay in seeking it because of something you have read in our material.

The resources provided are not designed to practice medicine or give professional medical advice, including, without limitation, medical direction concerning someone's medical and mental health. Any resources given are not to be considered complete and does not cover all issues related to mental and physical health. In addition, any information given should not replace consultation with your doctor or any other mental health providers and/or specialists.

INTRODUCTION
Start Here

You are most likely reading this book because you are hungry for more. Or quite possibly, you just need some language or tools to process what you are going through.

Someone may have passed this book onto you with one of those, *"you really need this,"* kind of sentiments. Or with great skepticism, you've thought, *"Alright, what's this DeJesus guy got to say about the heart?"*

Whatever the reason, I'm glad you are giving this book a shot. I find that many of our life experiences call us to dig deeper, past surface living and lifeless routines into greater meaning. You were meant for a healed and free lifestyle. Quite often, it just takes a little more fruitful digging.

I have hungered for a richer and deeper existence my whole life. But for so long, I didn't know what to do with what was going on in my heart. I had no clue how to process some of my emotions or get to the bottom of my daily battles.

Maybe you are in the same boat or can relate to some of these statements:

- You are tired of going through the motions in life. You want to know how to live fully alive from the heart.
- You want to make sense of your past experiences so that you can live a more fulfilling future.

- You have heard enough messages that address the heart from a condemning and religiously legalistic perspective.
- You are weary of feeling guilty that you are never doing enough.
- You want to have more heart connected experiences with God and others.

Jesus came to bring us life to the fullest, yet that life must be fully experienced from the heart He gave you. Yet it's been my observation that many believers do not know how to live an abundant life from the heart. Our fatigue, weariness and numbed-out existence tell us something is off.

I have spent many years helping people, often being called into some of the most challenging situations. With first-hand experience, I have rolled up my sleeves addressing emotional breakdowns, church crisis issues, leadership failings and problems in the home.

Throughout this journey, I have wasted plenty of time chasing down symptoms with little to no fruit. It wasn't until I began to discern patterns and needs of the heart that everything began to change. My personal work with people began to accelerate. But most of all, I found myself free to live abundantly from my heart.

This book is not about my arrival, but my passionate journey of experiencing greater love, joy and peace through actually allowing my heart to process healing and freedom. Some areas of my heart needed rebuilding; other areas required a whole new foundation.

That may sound overwhelming to some, but heart healing should be simple. This book is about simplicity, but please hear me out, it's not necessarily about ease. It can be tough, even painful. But the end result is always a heart that is more alive and awake to life. On the other side of heart renovations are greater peace and joy.

My prayer for this book is that you will:

- Recognize the need for your heart to experience continued healing.

- Allow yourself to engage an effective, yet practical heart healing journey.
- Gain simple, yet profound precepts that will jump-start your heart.
- Breakthrough hindrances or questions that keep you stuck.
- Address unresolved issues of your life with greater love and clarity.
- Engage a lifestyle that lives from a more healthy and whole heart.
- Empower more vulnerable and authentic relationships around you.

I spend my life learning, researching and personally practicing the precepts of heart transformation. Nothing in this book is theory. It's been hard tested in the trenches. My wife and I have experienced tremendous freedom from struggles we thought we'd always have to tolerate. At the same time, we've had areas that tested us to the core, causing us to dig deeper in what we needed to learn and grow in.

So, with joy, we share what we've learned; most of it coming through times of struggle, pain and resistance. Yet there is one thing we know for certain: ***there is hope for your heart to experience greater healing and transformation.***

I ask that you take your time and open your heart as you read. I am not as concerned about feeding you information as I am about sharing insights that will speak to and awaken your heart. I am not as interested in making you smarter, where you can impress people with your knowledge. It's my dream to enhance the life of your heart, so that when people spend time with you, they are forever blessed because of crossing paths with who you are.

My prayer is that God will breathe life and healing to your heart as well as teach you to transform the ways you think. When your heart comes alive with truth, look out world!

See you on the journey.

01:
TENDING TO YOUR GARDEN

And even now the ax is laid to the root of the trees. Matthew 3:10a

I grew up in the city and had little access to any kind of yard. Therefore, I didn't have much experience with yard work or gardening. Today, I can appreciate a good couple of hours working outside in the sun and tending to a garden or yard. I am becoming more passionate about what it takes to landscape and care for the soil.

When my family recently moved from Connecticut to North Carolina, we were able to have a home with a yard that needed lots of manicuring and maintenance. With this transition, blossomed a passion in both my wife and I to get outside as much as possible to clean up, plant and care for the property. As a result, we have learned to appreciate a well-kept yard, especially because we get to watch our children enjoy it.

Whether you enjoy the process of working in a yard or not, caring for plants and soil takes persistent investment. You cannot automate the process by setting the soil and expect to arrive a few months later with a harvest. If you want strong crops, consistent attention, investment and maintenance must be cultivated. Ensuring that proper sunlight gets to the plants, while daily watering them is a must.

In addition to that, becoming aware of weeds that seek to encroach on your soil is critical to the health of the land. When we first moved in, we spent hours and hours removing weeds and brush that had been ignored and consumed the yard. It was our job to clean them out and keep them out.

Weeds are an interesting phenomenon. They grow subtly, but at the same time, quickly. Over time, weeds can hold your entire garden hostage. I find that I can look at a spot in my yard and see weeds growing there that I did not notice a couple days earlier. As soon as you cut one weed, another grows in its place. Although there are a number of ways to rid your garden of invading weeds, there is nothing more effective than tearing out a weed by the root system.

TAKE A DEEPER LOOK

What is true in the natural world is true for your spiritual and emotional journey. In the garden of your life grow various thoughts, beliefs and actions on a daily basis. Take a deeper look into the root system and you will find the core of your entire life. It's called your heart.

All of life flows from the heart. Whether you tend to your heart or not, the main thrust of all that you do flows from what is cultivated or not cultivated there. The heart is the control center for everything that grows and does not grow. It determines the quality of the soil and the root system that is produced in the garden of your life.

When your heart experiences change, everything is impacted. But you must be willing to get to the root issues of your life, otherwise you will spin in circles and repeat the same problems continually.

ADDRESSING THE ROOT SYSTEM OF YOUR HEART

You and I both know that nothing changes unless we get to the root of the problem. A weed cannot be eradicated unless you pull it out by the root. A disease cannot be treated effectively unless you deal with the root cause. A bad habit cannot be changed permanently unless you get to the core issue that needs to be addressed.

You have to get to the root if you want to grow healthy fruit in your life.

We know this in theory, but we often run from the root issues in our heart that need attention. We miss getting to the core issues, because they involve addressing the motives and broken patterns that drive us into disempowering ruts.

On top of that, we focus so much on symptoms that we miss the core issues that may be fueling our broken manifestations. We're asking God to move us into new places, provide for our needs and give us an abundant life, yet we neglect to deal with the weeds in our garden that may be preventing a full life from manifesting.

WHEN THE WEEDS SHOW UP

The weeds do not show up right away in our hearts. They take time to fester and grow. Down the road, the weeds show up through some of our negative life experiences. Certain agreements enter our heart where we slowly come into alignment with thoughts that condition us to become fearful, condemned, bitter, critical, negative or hardened.

Remember, this doesn't happen overnight, but the weeds will build momentum to entangle and choke the fruit you were made to produce.

Weeds can manifest in a myriad of ways, yet in our panic, we want to "fix" the weeds without getting to the real problem. We focus our attention on the branches and entanglements that the weeds produce. But we neglect to discover the root system feeding those weeds.

We see a list of manifestations that are actually revealing a deeper issue:

- *I have a thought pattern I can't shake.*
- *I am addicted and can't stop.*
- *My marriage is on the rocks.*
- *Why am I always so angry?*
- *I think I might be depressed.*
- *My heart feels so empty.*
- *I'm lonely.*
- *I can't get over this anxiety.*
- *My life feels out of control.*
- *I'm burned out.*
- *I can't seem to keep it together.*

It's good that you can stop to realize there is a problem, but you can really miss out on dynamic transformation if you are only focused on symptoms. We have to get to the root system. We need to get to your heart.

YOUR HEART NEEDS HEALING

Sometimes the most obvious things we need seem hidden, even though they are in plain sight. Most of the solutions for our life are very simple, yet often ignored. One of the greatest practices that is neglected is the need to cultivate and care for the life of the heart.

Sin has definitely infected our hearts with various forms of brokenness. But the fact that we overlook the issues of the heart, keep us in a shallow lifestyle, without depth in our transformational experiences.

We are broken people living in a broken world, attempting to live meaningful lives. But we are often so unaware of how our brokenness affects us. In addition, we're so scared of letting our vulnerabilities show. Life and the enemy have trained us to hide our brokenness at all costs. Meanwhile, the brokenness is festering and having a relational impact.

Can we all just admit that each of us have various areas of brokenness in our lives? If we can get honest that we are all broken to some degree, then we would have a lot more effective conversations and experience more authentic transformation.

THE MYTH MANY CHRISTIANS BELIEVE

Despite what many say, becoming a Christian does not make your brokenness completely disappear. In fact, a major aspect of maturing involves allowing God to heal the broken areas of our lives and establish greater levels of wholeness in our hearts.

Pursuing spiritual growth while ignoring underlying brokenness is like walking on a treadmill while eating a bowl of fries and a milkshake. You're not going to experience what's possible. Many are asking God to grow them, while at the same time, neglecting to address key issues of their heart.

For many, the process of sanctification is a revolving door that never changes. A lot of this has to do with the fact that brokenness of the heart has not been a priority in Christian growth.

When Jesus ministered, He often bypassed the small talk of symptoms and cut right to the root issue. He always pointed to the heart. In fact, His focus began with healing to the heart.

But relax and take a deep breath, because healing of the heart is a journey--an ongoing process more than just a one-time event. You and I are on a lifelong journey of allowing God to heal, renew and transform our hearts in powerful ways.

HEALING IS AVAILABLE TO YOUR HEART

The Gospel is good news from a good God, who loves you. But that love is meaningless if it is not received. Your heart was made to live in the power of love. Wherever God's love and nature is not received and experienced, brokenness dwells. We as human beings carry brokenness for a number of reasons:

1. Once sin infected the planet, our hearts became contaminated with broken thinking, belief systems and broken relationships.
2. Life experiences have wounded us, leaving us with broken mindsets and patterns that keep us in cycles of dysfunction.
3. We have deep emptiness, as a result of not being filled with the love we were designed to experience.
4. We all have areas of our heart that God's love and nature have not invaded yet. We all need deeper experiences with various aspects of Father God's character.

Recognizing your brokenness does not mean you walk around all day discouraged and living out a disempowered life. Quite the opposite. Recognizing your brokenness can be incredibly empowering; especially because of the humble posture it produces in you. You can become more teachable, moldable and able to receive the insight you need.

When you walk around like your garbage doesn't stink, it distances you from what you need. It will also make you live a fabricated life, while becoming more religiously legalistic towards others. People not recognizing their own brokenness is the reason we are all so hard on each other.

Heart healing does not lead us to a one-time event, but a continual growth process, that is why I am pointing you to the heart healing *journey*. Once we give our hearts permission to experience more of Christ's nature, we give God room to lead us on a whole new journey and lifestyle.

I invite you to give yourself permission and join me on this heart healing journey.

QUESTIONS FOR CONSIDERATION:

1. What areas of your life reveal there are some broken aspects of your heart?

2. What keeps you from admitting to personal brokenness in areas of your life?
3. Of the four reasons we are broken that I listed, which one stuck out to you the most?
4. After reading this chapter, what area of your heart is God speaking to?

PRAYER:

Father God, I come to You in Jesus name. I am beginning to recognize there are areas of my heart that need healing. I want to live in a way that cultivates a healthy life from the heart. I give You permission to lead me into a heart healing journey. Give me wisdom and insight as I learn to address the issues of my heart that need attention.

I desire to live a life that is healed and free. I am grateful that You sent Jesus to heal the broken heart. You have given us the invitation to live an abundant life from the heart. Your compassion, grace and kindness make this process possible, so I thank You for that.

I know that living a life from a heart that is free will bring about great fruit, so I give You permission to work on my heart. Lead me into the everlasting way. Walk with me and show me what I need to see. My heart is excited about the greater healing and freedom I will experience.

I thank You for it. In Jesus name I pray, amen.

02:
How's Your Heart?

for man looks at the outward appearance, but the Lord looks at the heart.
1 Samuel 16:7b

A question that is not commonly asked, but can be most revealing is, *"How is your heart doing these days?"*

First off, most people would not even know how to answer this question. Many would think you are asking about their cardiovascular status, while others would awkwardly look down and quickly ponder an answer that can help them escape the discomfort they feel.

But what most of us do is scan a list of other questions we think are tied to the *"how's your heart"* question. They reveal what we spend most of our attention, focus and investment on:

- *How much money am I making? How is business?*
- *Am I looking successful?*
- *Is my religious performance looking good?*
- *How does our family look to everyone?*
- *How are my social media interactions going?*
- *Is my ministry work getting a lot of positive feedback?*
- *How good do I look in a bathing suit? Have I lost the weight I want to lose?*
- *Are my kids involved in lots of activities and showing that I am a good parent?*
- *How do I look as I am answering this question?*

These questions lead us on a trail to nowhere, linking us to values that don't enhance the life of our hearts. They also tie us to a standard that is not based on what God sees as important.

But let's be honest, we spend a lot of time invested in activities that keep us busy, but don't exactly add value and life to our hearts. If you are not aware, you will live your life pursuing certain aims that carry their share of importance, but over time, will keep you from what really matters in the heart.

We know our lives are not perfect, but yet we invest so much energy making them look perfect, comparing ourselves to shallow standards and sacrificing blood, sweat and tears to factors that imprison us more than empower us.

More people are getting honest with their imperfect life, but at the same time, cannot see the beauty of what's possible right in the front of them. The broken areas of their heart have cultivated a disempowering perspective. Therefore, they cannot see the treasured relationships they can connect to, the preciousness of who they are and most of all, the infinite depths they can experience with God.

But most of all, too many are just settling. We settle for the shallow end and do the least amount possible, so we can just "get by."

Too many responses to *"how is your heart doing"* are often shallow and far from what the life of the heart is all about. We mean well, but it's easy to live all day from the shallow end, without giving room for questions that move us into a deeper life.

- *Have I been able to receive love today?*
- *Am I able to sense God's love for me?*
- *Am I making time to experience love, joy and peace?*
- *Am I aware of the predominant feelings I am experiencing?*
- *Am I dealing with pain in life effectively?*

- *Is my heart alive and fulfilled?*
- *How are my relationships? Am I connecting to God and people in meaningful ways?*
- *What's God saying to me in this season?*

By no means am I encouraging you to go into a cave, stare at the wall and live an introspective life. That's not healthy either. But what I am concerned about is how easy it can be to walk through life without much assessment for the life of your heart.

GETTING TO THE HEART

For where your treasure is, there your heart will be also. Matthew 6:21

My invitation to you is this: make a decision to live more from the treasured seat of your life--your heart. When your heart is addressed, you get to the real issues that motivate and influence your entire life. The heart is where your root system lies. If I find your heart, I'm going to discover all the things that are important to you, the issues that grip you and the values that motivate everything. When you live from the heart, life gets real, experiences become authentic and you find yourself becoming more fulfilled, day by day.

Everything Jesus did on this earth addressed the life of the heart. To this day, He is still all about having a heart exchange with you. He knows that if He can connect with your heart, He will have access to all that you are and be able to transform your life.

But isn't that the battleground? We struggle in wondering what Jesus will actually do if we open up to Him.

Behold, I stand at the door and knock. If anyone hears My voice and opens the door, I will come in to him and dine with him, and he with Me.
Revelation 3:20

What will Jesus do if we really open our hearts to Him? In this biblical passage, our Lord is not addressing unsaved people. He's talking to the church, inviting them into a new level of intimacy. This invitation is simple, yet powerful. All He wants to do is sit down and have a meal with you.

This meal speaks of intimate exchange and meaningful connection. But for so long, we have been avoiding this. Maybe because you thought when you open the door, God would body slam you and shout at all the things that are wrong with you. Quite possibly, you are not used to a relationship with someone where all they want to do is connect. Relational intimacy may be a foreign concept to you.

GOD IS ALL ABOUT THE HEART

Our Father in Heaven and our Lord Jesus want to have a real relationship with you. But you can only experience this if you are willing to have a real heart to heart relationship.

When you have a heart to heart relationship with God:

1. The highest value is relationship, more than religious duties, performance evaluations and task-focused living.
2. You give God permission to have access into every facet of your heart and life.
3. Your pace of life is not at hyper speed. There is a healthy rhythm and room on the edges of life for reflection.
4. You tune into allowing God to mature and develop your emotions, so you can become more emotionally present, engaged and empowered with God and others.
5. You understand that past experiences can have an impact on your present reality, so you allow God to bring healing to those areas that can become hindrances.
6. You allow symptomatic problems in your life to lead you towards letting God teach you about the motives and beliefs of the heart that drive those behaviors and struggles.
7. You learn to receive from God, so that you have much to give others in the power of His love.

8. You recognize that God uses your earthly relationships to mature your life and even enhance your relationship with Him.

Sadly, it's not a surprise that most people have not been mentored in this. We therefore avoid issues of the heart like the plague, afraid we will be shamed and pushed into a corner to cry in endless pain.

And yet this is not true. Engaging a heart-to-heart experience with God leads us into an adventure like we've never known. You may feel some pain, but that's the whole point. You finally get to truly *feel* and awaken to what's possible.

MOVING PAST SYMPTOMS

Moving into a more heart connected journey starts by moving past surface evaluations and into more honest assessment. Dealing with the heart moves us past symptoms and to the real reasons why we do what we do; and especially why we do what we *don't* want to do.

Think of the many things you involve yourself with on a daily basis. Are you aware of the motives that drive your actions? It's easy to quickly assign noble intentions on many things that we do, without being aware of the broken motives we carry.

For example, you may be involved in helping people in some form or fashion. You communicate to everyone that you just love pouring out to others and showing love. While this is true, have you considered your unmet need to be validated and accepted that drives you to work endlessly on those projects? Is there a chronic busyness that keeps you from noticing the ache in your heart that is still empty?

What about those areas you're trying to break? Do you understand what's underneath the pornography addiction you can't seem to overcome? Or the anxiety that doesn't relent? What's going on with this depression or the anger that lashes out a little more often than you'd like?

This isn't a pop quiz or an interrogation, so don't worry. But it's time we invite God to reveal what's underneath these symptomatic problems, so that we become more in tune with what's happening inside.

ADDRESSING OUR DULL HEARTS

The good news is that when you have a heart experience with God, everything comes into an alignment with a different kind of journey. Connection with Him becomes personal, more than just routine or intellectual. Experiences become more meaningful, because you are communing with a God who is personal and real to your every move.

Many people are content with just getting smarter in knowledge. Yet they don't realize in the pursuit of knowledge as the highest aim, we can become dull in our hearts. Jesus addressed this to the generation of His day:

> *'Hearing you will hear and shall not understand,*
> *And seeing you will see and not perceive;*
> *For the hearts of this people have grown dull.*
> *Their ears are hard of hearing,*
> *And their eyes they have closed,*
> *Lest they should see with their eyes and hear with their ears,*
> *Lest they should understand with their hearts and turn,*
> *So that I should heal them.'*
> Matthew 13:14-15

This is the main reason why Jesus spoke in parables. He used the power of stories to draw in those who were seeking with their whole heart. Those who listened to Jesus, looking for quick information, "Three Steps to Life Change" or a form of theological knowledge they could impress someone with, were highly disappointed. In fact, they were often confused.

They didn't know how to engage the Kingdom of God with a full heart. Religion had trained them to place God in routine boxes that gave them a form of engaging God, but the power is filtered out.

FROM THEORY TO PERSONAL EXPERIENCE

Our current generation has the highest level of access to information and knowledge in the history of mankind. But our hearts are not improving in wisdom and depth. Our relationships reflect how little our hearts are healing and growing in wholeness.

Now don't misunderstand me. There is nothing wrong with growing in knowledge. The problem is, we live in a generation that is saturated with data, information and opinions, with little experience of truth.

We can tell someone how to pray, even when we haven't experienced the power of prayer ourselves. It's easy to tell someone about the joy of the Lord, but when was the last time you lived in it? You can share with someone about any aspect of God, but have you experienced His nature in that way personally?

When you live from a heart that is experiencing God, you move from mental theory and into the heart encounter you were made for. If knowledge doesn't eventually lead you to deeper heart passion and fruitful experiences, you may become intellectually smart, but spiritually dormant. When truth is experienced in your heart, it becomes a part of who you are, not just something you can quote.

Truth is not embedded in your heart until it is activated through experience. When you take action and live out what you are learning, it will lead you to have the power of truth deeply rooted in your heart. Because of this, you often have to go through something in life to really experience the power of truth that can set your heart free.

HEART TRANSFORMATION

If the heart is not regularly cultivated in real and authentic relationships with God and others, mankind has a tendency to seek transformation by forcing the mind to cooperate. We attempt to "think" our way into transformation. Our focus moves more into performance, achievement and the application of data, more than leaning into relational wholeness.

Methods often feed a person with information, but can leave them without transformation. This has created a society that has theories about everything, but little experience about how to live life to the fullest. Mankind has learned to be content with knowledge that has no experience to galvanize it into our being.

If simply gaining more information would do the trick, then the smartest people in the world would have the most fruit in their life. But we all know this is not true.

The key to engaging the life of the heart is desire and belief. When we believe, we open up the power of faith to move our lives into powerful directions. Desire is the connection of an awakened heart for what is possible. When desire is dead, the heart goes cold. When belief is absent, the heart becomes hard.

If you don't have desire, ask God to restore it. If you struggle to believe, ask God to help you with your unbelief. This comes down to a place of choice. Only you can decide to move the life of your heart into a renewed direction. God will meet you, but you have to make the choice to yield to His supernatural power.

QUESTIONS FOR CONSIDERATION:

1. If someone was to ask you *"How is your heart doing?"* and this was a safe person to talk to, what would you say? What would be the predominant theme that your heart needs to address right now?

2. In what area of your life do you need to move past just surface living and get to the heart of what is going on?

3. What is an area that you need to grow more in "heart understanding," not just having knowledge in your head about it?

4. When it comes to desire and belief, which one do you need to address today?

PRAYER:

Father God, I do not want to just know about You, I want to know You and experience who You are with my whole heart. I ask that You help me to move from just mind knowledge and learn to engage who You are and experience the power of Your nature. Unclog my ears and open my eyes, so that I may receive the power of true heart healing and transformation.

Reveal the beliefs I carry which are hindering my walk with You and other people. Expose the lies so that I may experience truth in greater fullness.

Restore desire in my heart. Meet me in my disappointments and sorrow. Let my heart be mended and built up in the strength You have for me. I thank You for Your love. Today I ask that You lead me into a path that experiences that healing love.

In Jesus name, amen.

03:
The Foundation is Cracked

...you are God's building. According to the grace of God which was given to me, as a wise master builder I have laid the foundation, and another builds on it. But let each one take heed how he builds on it.
1 Corinthians 3:9-10

It is amazing what God can do while you are working a job you did not expect to have. For me, it was construction work. I had very little experience in this area, so I had to learn fast. My family and I found ourselves in financial hard times, so I had to take advantage of the jobs that were available. Working for friends who were in the construction business would usher in some of the greatest learning I've ever had, though most of it was delivered in unexpected ways. Some of the biggest hardships in life can be the greatest places for God to work as a Master Craftsman on our hearts.

Some construction projects were brand new homes, while others were renovations. As I labored in the day to day grind, I sought to learn as much as possible. One thing I quickly observed was how important the foundation was to the rest of the structure. In fact, as I was working on these houses, I sensed that God was simultaneously renovating my own spiritual foundation. It was time for God to do some work on my heart. Having to work these jobs was a massive lesson of humility, so He had my undivided attention.

There are many times in life where the issues we face are actually a call to go deeper, to get to the groundwork of our hearts. During this season of my life, I wanted God to open doors and lead me into new and exciting ventures. But all the signs kept pointing me back to what I saw on those construction sites: *the foundation needs more attention.*

Everything I was going through was a call for me to address the foundational issues of the heart that can get so easily ignored or neglected, yet they influence everything in life. So, in order for me to experience the greater life I longed for, I had to give God permission to renovate the foundation.

You and I can get easily overwhelmed by the complexity that our battles bring. It seems there is so much drama, frustration and confusion that accumulates in our journey. One big reason for this is that we are not equipped to address our foundation. We keep attacking symptoms while neglecting the simple, yet foundational issues that need a renovation.

Now when I say, simple, don't hear me wrong. I don't mean easy. Heart renovation takes time, patience and investment. But the solutions you need are often so simple, they can pass you by if you are not paying attention.

The key is that you need an open and teachable heart. In other words, you just need to be ready. My circumstances humbled me to the point that I was ready for whatever God needed to do in my heart.

ALLOWING FOR THE "GUT JOB"

Back to the construction site. When working on home renovations, it was rare that simple fixes would suffice. Usually a "gut job" was needed, especially because the structural issues behind the symptomatic problems needed to be addressed. I was deeply impacted by something I took for granted: *you cannot casually pass the foundational stages.* The foundation is everything.

I found many parallels to our spiritual life and the dilemma that exist within modern Christianity. We often lack a solid foundation in our spiritual life. Because of this, cracks and instability are manifesting in so many areas of our lives. Yet, in our search for repair, we often fail to have our spiritual foundation examined.

When someone comes to me for personal help, there are usually symptomatic issues they are hoping to address. An addiction has taken over, their marriage is on the rocks, struggles of the mind seem to be dominating, a workplace problem seems to be holding them back or they simply can't get over a hurt from the past. They may be looking for help regarding depression, anxiety or anger battles.

These struggles are all subjects that call us to address the underpinning issues that need attention. The problem is that most of our life pattern has been conditioned to patch holes in the walls of our hearts as much as possible. *"Put a quick band aid on this and get on with life"* seems to be the theme most people live by.

Yet as the footings of our hearts keep getting ignored, we ask ourselves the same questions over and again:

- *Why does this issue keep rising up?*
- *Why am I so unhappy?*
- *Why can't I catch a break?*
- *Why am I leaning into that fourth glass of wine?*
- *Why am I so obsessed with what's going on at work?*
- *What's up with this anxiety I'm feeling?*
- *Why do I feel so angry?*
- *Why do I feel so awful, sick and worn out?*

Until we are willing to ask better questions and face the foundational issues of our hearts, we will always be patching holes that keep leaking.

THE LONGING FOR TRANSFORMATION

For many, there is a cry for transformation, a desire to experience healing and freedom in their hearts. We want a fruitful walk with God, a strong sense of who we are and better relationships.

Yet the road of transformation is filled with resistance, roadblocks and unwanted detours that often seek to derail our ability to live healed and free. This leaves many in a world of "status quo," where life does not seem to change, they feel stuck and hearts begin to lose steam. Others settle for a mundane and lifeless existence.

Many of the issues of the heart can easily bury themselves, so it often takes certain symptomatic issues to get our attention. Your wife tells you if you don't get help, she's leaving. You find yourself drinking way too much. Pornography has become an easy lure. Anxiety seems to be increasing and unrelenting. Your health is waning because the stress and internal conflicts are taking a toll on your physiology.

It took a personal breakdown in my life for me to come face to face with the obstacles that were preventing me from wholeness. I had blaring issues I needed to confront, but like many, I was able to avoid them on a day to day basis. Anxiety, obsessive compulsive patterns, panic attacks and depression were pummeling me like a category five hurricane.

As many do, I spent a lot of time trying to patch holes, looking for quick fixes, until I made the decision to let God repair the foundations of my heart. No chasing symptoms anymore. It was time for me to get to the root issues of my life. This new perspective permanently changed my life trajectory. When it came to my personal growth and the ministry of helping others, I was no longer satisfied with surface Christian living.

EMBRACING THE "EVERYTHINGS"

The Kingdom of God is built upon key foundations. They cannot be rushed through and must be continually revisited. Upon these foundations, the precepts of God and His ways are built. My wife and I call them the *"everythings"* because they are important in the beginning and must be cultivated all throughout life. They are subjects you never leave behind.

We found that calling them the *"everythings"* reminds us to continually grow and mature in these areas; never thinking we have fully arrived. They need to be cultivated during our entire life and involve three major subjects that impact everything else:

1. How you relate to God.
2. How you see yourself.
3. How you interact with the world around you.

So, let me get brutally honest. Many believers say they know *about* the love of God, but cannot honestly remember the last time they personally experienced that love. We sort of know what forgiveness is, yet we default to anger, gossip and resentment constantly. We hate being judged and condemned, yet we throw stones at people all the time.

We all have struggles in our mental and emotional worlds, yet we find ways to cover them up. Our insecurities, jealousy issues and fears hide underneath a layer of shame that keeps us from experiencing the healing we were designed for.

At the same time, we are tirelessly busy, with no end in sight. Yet we keep our lives filled with activities, most of which provide no life to the heart. For most, it seems better to fill in the spare moments of the day, so we don't have to stop and face what's really going on. The emptiness is too painful to face.

Peace and joy are our birthright, but the majority of problems we are facing seem to steal our ability to experience it. Our relationships are strained and dysfunctional, but we don't know how to move deeper into real and authentic connection. We're motivated more by fear in most settings than we'd like to admit.

In my journey of heart renovation, I felt God speak to me this thought: *You need to live and dwell in the basics. Get back to the foundation. They are the everythings.*

GO BACK TO THE BEGINNING

In the book of Revelation, Jesus handed out one of His most challenging rebukes to a church that had lost touch with an important foundational heart issue. Amidst all their achievements, riches and success they touted, our Lord called out something of value that was missing, an issue of the heart they needed to get awakened to.

Even though the Laodicean church may have appeared to be successful, Jesus saw them headed for destruction, simply because they lost the importance of passionate heart connection. As a result, they accepted a lifestyle that made our Savior's stomach turn. He called it lukewarmness.

Things may look great on the outside. But the truth is, they tolerated a lifeless form of religiosity that kept them busy, but left them no longer heart connected.

So then, because you are lukewarm, and neither cold nor hot, I will vomit you out of My mouth.
Revelation 3:16

A lifestyle that is lukewarm nauseates God, but it doesn't seem to bother a lot of people. It is amazing how we can make peace with a life that is passionless; with little attention given to it.

Lukewarmness puts us into a spiritual and emotional coma, yet on the outside, we can still go through the motions. Jesus' words are calling us today to wake from our slumber and shake out the spiritual lukewarmness that has conditioned our hearts into a powerless life.

Jesus told another church that they had left the world of passionate heart love:

Nevertheless, I have this against you, that you have left your first love.
Revelation 2:4

From the outside, the church of Ephesus had everything going on. They were the growing and productive body of believers. They manifested church success in so many ways. Yet at the same time, Jesus needed to address an issue of the heart. They left "first love" living. The foundation was cracked.

So, the remedy that Jesus provided still echoes today. *Go back. Get back to the precept you either forgot or skipped over. Turn and go back to the beginning.*

Remember therefore from where you have fallen; repent and do the first works, or else I will come to you quickly and remove your lampstand from its place—unless you repent.
Revelation 2:5

Pretty strong words, but that's what Jesus always delivers. He cuts past what most people focus on and He dives right into the heart, while loving you throughout it all with undying affection and grace. This strikes many in uncomfortable ways, because they are not used to being simultaneously loved and disciplined. Jesus is shaking our hearts for what matters most--a heart fully alive to Him.

If you read through this exhortation and feel you need to do more tasks and engage more religious activity, you missed the entire point. Heart connection is not about performance, it's about relationship cultivation, where you guard the value of receiving and living from the refreshment of loving connection with your Creator.

A NEW DIRECTION

My struggles led me to a life changing series of actions that I want to share with you today. If you want to live a heart-connected lifestyle, here are some things to ponder:

1. Make a clear decision.

Are you willing to give God your full heart, while living a life that is more heart connected? This must be a clear decision, followed by action. You cannot "half" your way into this and it's a decision that only you can make for yourself.

2. Be honest with yourself.

This means no more playing games or dancing around the issues that are affecting your heart and life. What's the deeper call in your heart that God is bringing you into? As you get honest with God, who in your life do you need to get more honest with about your own healing journey?

As you do this, keep in mind that it is possible to be honest with yourself without shaming yourself. Nothing sabotages the work of God more than self-condemnation and self-contempt. We cannot experience heart freedom while beating ourselves up at the same time. It's like putting your accelerator to the floor with the emergency break all the way on.

One of the reasons many do not deal with the core issues of their heart is because they feel a boatload of shame whenever they open up that subject of brokenness and pain. Their inspection is done with eyes of disgust rather than love and grace.

With a perspective of love and grace, you can face any issue of your heart. You'll know that no matter what you've done or gone through, you are loved.

3. Humble yourself.

Transformation is not about how smart or spiritual you seem to be. It's all about whether your heart carries humility. Are you teachable? Do you make others feel safe around you? Can you learn from others? Do you present yourself as arriving and not needing any healing? Or do you acknowledge that you are in process just like everyone else?

Sometimes the first step of humility is acknowledging to God and those close to you that there are issues of your heart that need attention, healing and growth. God is pouring out grace to the humble. But he resists the proud all day long.

God resists the proud, but gives grace to the humble. 1 Peter 5:5

Humility starts with vulnerability and teachability. Most people don't stick around long enough to be taught in the areas they really need to address. They may sit under a teacher, mentor or coach for a short time but as soon as things get challenging, they withdraw and move on. It reveals a limitation that needs to be faced.

4. Keep it simple.

Heart healing and transformation point us to the simple things-- foundational areas that need time to develop. I have spent years in introspection, wondering if there was a super deep and hidden issue that I needed to uncover. I wondered if I was able to uncover this mysteriously hidden issue, maybe I would discover my silver bullet of freedom.

And yet I found that there was no hidden issue. They were all right in front of me; mostly in plain sight. I just needed to be willing to address them and give myself time to learn. I believe the same is true for you, if you will make the decision to open your heart and allow God to clear up your eyesight.

QUESTIONS FOR CONSIDERATION:

1. In what area or areas are you longing for deep transformation?

2. Where do you have a tendency to do "patch work" over your heart, while neglecting the renovation that's needed?

3. Where do you find yourself "leaving your first love" or becoming lukewarm? What one thing do you sense God calling you to, in order to experience change?

4. Of the closing steps suggested, which one do you need to put into action today?

PRAYER:

Father, I am grateful that You want transformation for my heart and life. It is Your desire to see me live free and to have a life that is abundant. I am realizing that in order to experience the freedom my heart longs for, I need to let You address the foundational issues of my heart.

So, I make a decision today to allow You into my heart. I receive the work of Christ with my whole heart. I say yes to His death and resurrection. I open my heart to a new and refreshed journey. I go back to the foundation and give You room to renew and transform me. Father, I give You access to the places of my heart that need Your love, truth and grace in a dynamic way. Teach me, lead me and show me the way.

Help me to get honest with You and even honest with myself, so that I may deal with the issues of my heart that need healing. Help me to humble myself, so that I may learn from You and position my heart to experience Your power in every area of my life. I humble myself before You God and allow you to do the renovation You need to do in my heart.

I rejoice in what lies ahead and I trust that You will lead me each step of the way.

In Jesus name, amen.

04:
Recovering Your Footing

Remember therefore from where you have fallen; repent and do the first works…
Revelation 2:5a

If you were to get lost in the woods, the best thing to do is retrace your steps. You may need to simply find where you went off track so you can regain your footing and sense of direction. The same is true in your heart healing journey. You need to first realize that you've lost your way, while retracing your steps back to the solid path.

To use the words of Jesus, we need to "repent and go back to the first works." In order to live a more healed and free life from the heart, we need to direct our hearts to the right path. This will involve turning around, going back and retracing some steps that need to be addressed.

That's what repentance is. Don't be confused by images of people groveling in never ending tears and unproductive penance. Real repentance involves a change of thinking into a new direction. God is giving our hearts a chance to go back and carve out a new direction as we engage the heart healing journey.

When Jesus made this statement of "repent and do the first works," He was not addressing unbelieving pagans. Nor was it given to brand new Christians. He gave this heart awakening charge to a well-seasoned, "leading the way" kind of church who had in fact, lost their way.

This should never be a word to condemn, but for strengthening the footings of God's work in your heart; to realign you with His priorities. For many, heart healing has been neglected all throughout life, so going back to the foundation may involve facing some broken perspectives, patterns of thinking and beliefs that need God's transformational work.

ADDRESSING THE FOUNDATION

When I engaged a heart healing renovation with God, it became clear to me that He was rebooting my spiritual life. I feel like I started my whole Christian walk over, so I could go back and experience the richness of what I often skipped over or missed completely.

In one hundred percent of the work I've done helping others navigate battles of the mind, habits they can't break or relationship challenges, there was always a foundational issue that had been neglected. It may be a pastor who has some deep addictions he can't seem to overcome. Maybe a dad is struggling with pornography or a mom is so emotionally worn out, she is numb. It could be a business leader who cannot shake the never-ending emptiness inside or a believer who has been battling depression and anxiety that doesn't stop.

In the midst of our struggles is a call to return to the issues that were skipped over or neglected for some time. When we lose track, we lose sight of the simple, basic foundations that are meant to uphold us. We forget the *everythings*.

Sometimes it helps to look back and see where things got off track and invite God into those places. It doesn't need to be complicated. No need for years of introspection. Sometimes it just requires humility, teachability and an authentic request for God's help.

I had a long season of breakdown that manifested in chronic anxiety, panic attacks and obsessive thinking. These battles revealed my need for reconstruction. I was a hot mess inside, but I neglected the inner work I needed for a while. It was only when I surrendered and humbled my heart, that I was able to hear God say, *Go back to the foundations. They are everything.*

Many precepts needed to be revisited, while other revelations needed to be formed in my life for the first time. I lost my way through losing sight of valuable truths, or because I never possessed them to begin with. Even though I grew up in church, there were many heart related subjects I simply never experienced.

Like many believers, I was faking my way through knowing the love of God and living secure in my identity. I never knew God's love for me as my Father. I had no clue who I was apart from all the busy religious activities I was involved in. Rejection issues lay deep within my broken heart. Yet I hid my self-hatred and insecurities like a professional. So, in reality, I was a performer, going through the motions with the impression that I possessed the things of God, when in reality, that was the furthest from the truth.

Because of this, we often need a "rock bottom" experience for us to awaken to our need for heart healing. The pain increasing or a crisis intensifies to arrest our attention to matters of the heart that have been neglected.

We all need help. Despite the mass of Christians on social media who act like they have arrived, there is no one who has completely mastered the *"everythings."* Anyone who comes across that way is self-deceived.

To the authentic believer, the *everythings* of the heart are always the headline subject. Each stage of life is meant to experience a new facet of the love and grace of God. This is meant to develop our identity, so that the world is impacted, not by our superior knowledge or impressive intellect, but by how deeply rooted we are as sons and daughters of God.

A CHANCE TO START OVER

But as you allow the renovation process to take shape, there are some powerful *"everythings"* to visit and revisit continually. One of those everythings is the opportunity to have a fresh start.

When Jesus arrives to awaken and heal your heart, He first begins by offering you a new heart to live from.

I will give you a new heart . . . Ezekiel 36:26

The power of the cross and resurrection provide us with an opportunity to receive a new start with a new heart. God ushers in a heavenly makeover. He's basically saying, *"We have to start this all over, right from the beginning."* God does not build on top of our broken upbringing; He starts us over so we can experience a whole new tutelage in living as a loved child.

That is why receiving Christ is called the "born again" experience. You go back to infancy and grow up again. This helps set the stage for what a heart connected life with Christ and the Father can be.

But how many believers have a solid reference for what it means to be loved as God's child? It has become so cliché that it is often skipped over as a subject which needs no further attention.

Quite the opposite. Being loved as God's child needs to be continually revisited. In fact, we will spend the rest of our lives learning to experience the Father's love, expressed through His Son, Jesus Christ. A life from the heart is a continual journey of discovering what it means to be unconditionally loved as a child, by a perfect Father in heaven.

When God gets a hold of our hearts, He initiates a heavenly reboot, so don't be surprised in your healing journey when God says,

"Let's go back to the beginning." Although this step seems like a setback in your journey, it is actually a giant leap forward in God's eyes.

God will often take us back to revisit Kingdom subjects that have become religious rituals, with little impact on our hearts. Sometimes it can be as simple as revisiting your born-again experience.

Living as a believer is more than just giving mental assent, saying a nice prayer or participating in religious duties. Our journey with God starts with a believing heart and continues as a heart journey. Many modern-day believers lose track when their Christian life becomes a mass list of sacred tasks and impressive theology they can quote with their minds, but have lost connection within their heart.

The greatest way we can reset our spiritual journey is to get back to the simplicity of believing and connecting from our hearts.

. . . if you confess with your mouth the Lord Jesus and believe in your heart that God has raised Him from the dead, you will be saved. For with the heart one believes unto righteousness, and with the mouth confession is made unto salvation.
Romans 10:9-10

BECOMING GOD'S CHILD

Behold what manner of love the Father has bestowed on us, that we should be called children of God!
1 John 3:1

One of the greatest treasures we have as believers is the opportunity to live as a loved child of our Father in heaven. Yet in the decades of rolling up my sleeves and working with the hearts of people, this precept is more a theory than reality for many. In fact, most of the battles believers face come out of feeling disconnected from the Father's love and not knowing who they are in their identity.

So, before you are tempted to rush and read on, honestly ask yourself, *"Do I really know what it means to live as a dearly loved child by my*

Father in heaven? Am I able to connect to that love right now? Do I live out of a confident identity as a son or daughter of God?"

Experiencing the Father's love is everything. His love tells you who you are and builds the confidence you need to live it out. A careful examination of the battles that believers face show there is a war over what love means and a fight to keep you from walking in the full expression of your eternal identity.

SONS AND DAUGHTERS

When we believe and receive Christ into our lives, we are given a brand-new identity: we are now sons and daughters of Father God. Anything else is just a cheap counterfeit. We are no longer just natural people with biological parents. We are spiritual sons and daughters of God. He is now our Father. We are now stamped as His dearly loved and treasured children!

The Spirit Himself bears witness with our spirit that we are children of God…
Romans 8:16

When God speaks to the hearts of believers, He communicates to us as sons and daughters, not as orphans or slaves. Sonship is a key foundation to a relationship with God because it establishes a true knowing of who we are. It also tunes our hearts into how God speaks to us. We cannot experience fruitful transformation apart from the relationship of a Father to a son.

So, it is important to ask yourself, *"Do I really know what it feels like to be totally and unconditionally loved by my Father in heaven? Am I immersed in His approval, validation and acceptance?"*

These questions identify a key place where satan attacks believers the most:

1. Keep God's children from connecting to the Father's love.
2. Prevent believers from walking in the power of their true identity.

People all over the planet are in a minute by minute battle over whether or not they are loved and accepted. For many of you, God wants to take you back to what it really means to be loved by Him. You will also need to strip off all the added layers that have piled up on your identity and revisit the simplicity of being loved as God's child. It's possible that Jesus needs to take you into His lap as He did those children and help you to realize, *"this is the Kingdom of heaven"* (Matthew 19:14).

TRUE INSIDE-OUT CHANGE

Love and identity are everything, because they set the template for all that God will do in your life. You no longer hide in shame, because you know His love and grace is present to work with you through every issue of your life. You learn to see that trials are a season for your relationship with Him to be strengthened. Your trust is empowered, because you know your Father in heaven is maturing you at every stage of life. With God's love imbedded in your heart, hope is strengthened and your faith builds confidence.

Transformation can be a waste of time if we are not building it on the Father's love. You will spend your life chasing symptoms or attempting to "will" yourself into change by performance-based living. You will also pile up a list of spiritual disciplines, while still feeling empty.

God wants to get to the root system of your life, but this cannot happen effectively, unless you know you are loved by Him. Love sets the foundation of trust, so that as He leads you into transformation, you know in your heart that all His motives towards you are good and for a good future.

QUESTIONS FOR CONSIDERATION:

1. What symptoms are showing up in life that reveal you need to retrace your steps and revisit some important "everythings?"
2. What precepts have you neglected that you need to return to?

3. If you are to be totally honest, what aspects of love and identity can you acknowledge that you've never received?

4. What's the biggest obstacle in your life that is preventing you from experiencing a true heart renovation with God?

PRAYER:

Father God, I thank You that the power of Your Kingdom is not complicated, nor too far out of reach. Your ways are higher than our ways, but You meet us in simplicity of heart connection. Thank You for Your grace and kindness towards me. Allow my heart to become aware of the things I need to return to, while also introducing me to important experiences with your love that I've never had.

Father, show me Your love. Help me to experience it. Allow the Scriptures to come alive in my heart, so that I can awaken to what's possible in my life. Help me to break through the fears, shame and stubbornness that keep me from receiving all that my heart can receive from You. I ask that in Your love, You help me to see who I am as Your child. Grow me to become rooted in the power of who You have called me to be. In Jesus name I pray, amen.

05:
Cultivating Heart Awareness

Keep your heart with all diligence, for out of it spring the issues of life.
Proverbs 4:23

Countless times, people have sat in my office or met with me over a call to work through a personal struggle in their life. One of the predominant patterns I have observed is that many are often unaware to how much certain life experiences have impacted them. They are furthermore unable to articulate or even connect to what is happening in the life of their heart.

We are often trained to put our heads down and plow forward like oxen. Yet, we shake our heads in wonder when unwanted symptoms arise, revealing something is "off" in our heart life. It is imperative that we learn to live a more awakened and alive existence. We cannot wait until we are manifesting mental breakdowns, relationship rifts, addictions or certain anger and anxiety symptoms that don't stop, to then start dealing with our hearts.

The key to this awakening involves becoming more heart aware, which can lead us into subjects of self-awareness, emotional intelligence and social development. I call it "heart awareness," because it comes down to seven key agreements for a believer:

1. "I value the life of the heart."

Those who possess strong heart awareness connect to life from the heart. They don't simply go through the motions or remain content with surface relationships. Shallow pursuits are not appealing. They long for real and authentic experiences that a relationship with God and others can bring.

2. "I am aware of how life experiences impact my heart."

Valuing the life of the heart means allowing yourself to connect to what your heart experiences. Heart awareness involves understanding how life events have impacted your thoughts and emotions. In order to become stronger in heart awareness, you need to be keen on how your thoughts and emotions have been influenced.

With this level of heart awareness, you understand how your history can have an impact on your present. This can only be understood in the context of God's love and grace, for without them, we immediately fall into the pits of guilt, shame and condemnation.

Heart healthy people have tasted of the safety that God's love brings. At the same time, they are able to process through aspects of their broken history that are infecting their present potential and maturity.

3. "I am aware of my heart's condition."

This involves a level of self-awareness, the ability to know what is going on in my heart and emotions, while also knowing how I come across to others.

When you are aware of your heart's condition, you are able to digest the themes that God is working on in your life. Healing and maturity are much more fruitful, because you have tapped into God's frequency over your life. You're aware of what you are battling, as well as connecting to what God is teaching you.

No one is a perfect expert, but those who are heart aware can discern what is going on in the life of their own heart. They can also articulate it with safe people in an effective way.

In working with people over the decades, I have clearly observed that our generations lack training on how to articulate what we are feeling inside. Feelings have been ignored as messy, complicated and hindering. Therefore, many have said, "So why even pay attention to them? What's the point?"

Many have worried that if they paid attention to their heart, then they would become an unstable, emotional mess. This belief led them into another problematic ditch—becoming disconnected from the life of the heart.

Heart awakening takes intentionality and investment. I have spent months with people working through being able to identify what they are going through emotionally. Some were raised to completely ignore their emotions, so they lived like zombies. Others were told to suppress anger, fear and depression. Therefore, they never knew what to do with them, until one day their emotions exploded.

I think our current culture reveals that proper emotional nurturing has not taken place. I have taken this urgency into my own parenting, where I believe it is at the utmost of importance for my children to understand what they are feeling, so they can work through their emotions and mature their emotional capacity. I've met masses of people, who, if they had that opportunity growing up, their life would be dramatically different.

4. "I am allowing God to have full access to my heart."

In Psalm 139, David is expressing a vast array of emotions to God, when suddenly, he takes a left turn into anger for his enemies. While he knew it was acceptable to express a spectrum of various emotions, David also knew that he could not experience a healthy heart without God's involvement. So, he says:

> *Search me, O God, and know my heart;*
> *Try me, and know my anxieties;*
> *And see if there is any wicked way in me,*
> *And lead me in the way everlasting.*
> Psalms 139:23-24

Heart aware people seek to connect with God in meaningful ways that are relational. They live in a daily rhythm that unites their heart to God, not just religious routines they can check off a list. They're looking to grow with God in meaningful ways that manifest an abundant life.

This can only occur when you allow God to have an "all access pass" to your heart. You've made a personal decision to allow for Him to lead you into healing and maturity with His love and truth. With this permission given, God can freely move to heal the root issues of your heart that need addressing.

5. "I am seeking for God to heal and mature my heart."

Heart awareness means that processing healing and maturity in your heart life is important to you. Therefore, you become aware of the themes that God is working on. You give your heart room and time to slow down and tune into the direction of God, through His Word and the whispers of His Spirit.

6. "I seek to fully experience life."

A heart that is awakened and aware knows the importance of experiencing life with your full heart. This means you are present in the moment, allowing yourself to feel and connect to the relationships in front of you and the experiences you have the opportunity to engage.

Those who are heart aware are always learning, therefore they are always growing. They've positioned themselves in a way that they connect from the heart and want to keep growing in what it means to live, *fully alive from the heart.*

7. "I value the health of my relationships."

More important than achievement, status and wealth, heart aware people value relationships as the highest priority.

Most people say they value relationships, but their lifestyle does not mirror that. When relationships are an important value, then your pace of life, investment of time and focus will make room for important relationships to flourish. This begins in your home and extends to those God has called you to impact.

When you value relationships, you take the time to consider how you come across to others. You desire to be a safe space for others to heal and grow. You seek to develop and enhance your relationship interactions, so that people can benefit from the growth that God is leading you into.

Spiritual growth is meaningless, unless it shows up in our day to day relationship interactions. That is the greatest fruit of a transformed life. Other people receive the blessing of the change you have experienced.

THE BLESSINGS OF HEART-AWARENESS

When you live in healthy heart awareness, there are some wonderful blessings that can take place.

1. Your relationship with God becomes an exciting journey.

A heart aware believer will let go of mundane, religious mediocrity and dive into the adventure of communing with a Loving Father.

2. Transformational fruit is so much greater.

A heart aware believer gets to experience growth every single day. While many tell the same stories and problems they did years ago, a heart aware believer is experiencing the blessing of ongoing growth and transformation.

3. You are able to relate and connect to people in powerful ways.

Heart aware believers are people that you want to be around. Their openness and sincerity draw you to them, because they cultivate emotional safety, with an invitation for you to experience an abundant life.

4. What you learn out of challenging life experiences becomes a help for others.

The suffering, struggles and trials lead you to experience depths in your heart you've never encountered. But those experiences stretch you and build a depth to your character that you can now offer to others as encouragement and an example for them to follow.

5. You are able to powerfully connect with others in what they are going through.

Without heart awareness, your ability to cultivate compassion and empathy will lack. Therefore, deep and meaningful, long-term relationships will become challenging. People without heart awareness are the worst to be around in times of struggle. They either say very awkward and unhelpful things, or their silence and passivity become excruciating. It simply reveals they have not processed through the life of their own heart. Or they may not have been through life long enough to understand pain, heartache and loss.

But a heart aware person, who has faced their own journey of struggle, can authentically bless others from a place of humility and true vulnerability.

QUESTIONS FOR CONSIDERATION:

1. Of the seven agreements for heart awareness, which statement do you feel runs strongest in your life?
2. Which one do you desire to grow in the most?
3. What would happen to your relationships if you developed a stronger heart awareness in your life?
4. What one heart aware blessing do you hope to manifest more in your life?

PRAYER:

Father God, I pray You give me a heart like David, where I can pour out my heart to You and connect to life from the heart. I ask that You show me where I can give You greater access to experience You and become more present in my day to day relationships.

I want to move past mundane living and experience my life more fully. So, I ask that You help me to cultivate greater heart awareness with You and in those relationships You have put into my life. It is my heart's desire to be a blessing to my world. Help me to put relationships in greater priority. Give me the wisdom to know how to apply this. In Jesus name I pray, amen.

06: Waking Up to Your Brokenness

The Lord is near to those who have a broken heart . . . Psalms 34:18a

Somehow in the history of Christian living, religious performance had a way of moving us out of heart connection and into a world of accumulating knowledge. Building intellect has become the main focus, where dissecting information and being able to quote data is a shining accomplishment.

We check off our devotion time, scour through books and attend conferences that condition us to think we "know" something because we heard about it. We display our seminary training and articulate our impressive theological answers, all without experiencing in our hearts what the knowledge points to.

It's sad but true. You can accumulate a mass of knowledge that you never experience. Therefore, you can live your whole life deceiving yourself and others that you possess something you don't. It's the difference between listening to someone who knows every fact about the moon and meeting a man who actually stepped foot on the moon. You and I will choose to hear from the second person every time.

SETTLING FOR A LESSER LIFE

We have settled for a less than authentic heart experience. In the meantime, most believers feel like hypocrites. They tell other people to practice and engage things they have not applied themselves. Ministry time becomes a performance moment to "put on" something that really isn't a part of our daily existence. Feeling like a fraud, we then crawl into a cave of self-condemnation.

Our lifestyles become cycles of burnout. We go from one lifeless routine to another, wondering why we have all these addiction issues and troubling thoughts we can't shake.

This is the problem that stirred our Savior's heart; calling the people to understand with their hearts and turn into a new direction.

Lest they should understand with their hearts and turn,
So that I should heal them.
Matthew 13:15

What is the result of someone who receives God's truth in their hearts? They turn into a life of receiving the healing God has for them.

Can I challenge you with a question? Is it possible that many believers have turned to Christ, but never let their hearts experience the healing they need to truly "understand" His ways? It's just a question. I am not trying to add a religious checkbox to your life. I'm only asking to challenge your journey into greater heart transformation.

THE RESULTS OF WEAK HEART MUSCLES

The way we often do life reveals that many of our spiritual heart muscles have not been exercised. It shows up in a variety of areas:

- We go through the motions week after week and become content with no passionate heart connection.

- When trials and challenges hit us like a flood, there is little reservoir to draw from.

- Life becomes passive, where we coast through and deal with very few issues of the heart.

- We know our relationship with God needs an adjustment, but we don't know what to do about it.

- There are areas of your marriage that need work, but you put off doing anything about it. You chose to not ask your wife how she's doing, because her answer will call for you to invest more into the marriage. So, you put it off. Besides, the game is about to come on television anyway.

- You've been told that there are some wounds in your life you should address, but you defend and find ways to skirt away from those subjects.

- You have a friend that you need to have a heart to heart conversation with, but you never do. So, the friendship just slowly dies.

- You feel yourself drawn to certain addictions and you feel guilty about it. But you haven't allowed yourself to see what's going on in your heart that makes you drawn to those things in the first place.

- You are burned out, but you've come to the conclusion that you'll always be in this vicious cycle.

AS THE HEARTS GOES - EVERYTHING GOES

I remember as a young man in ministry, hearing about this Scripture in Proverbs, which emphasized the importance of living from the heart.

> *Keep your heart with all diligence, for out of it spring the issues of life.*
> Proverbs 4:23

In addition to *keep* your heart, other translations say:

- *Guard* your heart . . .
- *Watch* over your heart . . .

But have we been taught what this looks like? How do we guard, keep and watch over our hearts? Because the way I learned about it growing up was not heart development. It was often a performance-based focus:

Don't do this.

Make sure you don't screw up.

Stay away from that sin, because it will mess up your life.

Although right and wrong needs to be taught, we were rarely ever equipped to address the issues of the heart that could lead us into the wrong places.

Furthermore, why are so many Christians, who have served God most of their life, all of a sudden becoming jaded, hardened and even unbelieving? Did they wake up one day and decide they weren't going to believe anymore? Did this happen overnight? Or are there deeper issues of the heart that were neglected over time?

Why is it that a large number of Christians, who've been believers for decades, seem more worn out and cynical than ever before? Shouldn't we be developing, improving, growing and showing greater fruit as the years go by? Did this happen because a person stopped serving on the usher team, or is it really because issues of the heart were never addressed and nurtured?

Why do people fall into sexual temptation? It always seems to shock us when marriages are destroyed, or some kind of sexual sin is revealed. Is it because lust fell upon someone out of thin air? Or are there deeper issues of the heart that made way for the forbidden desires to manifest?

Could it be that we are stuck in the dilemmas we face, simply because our hearts are not receiving the healing we so desperately need?

THE HEART CONNECTION

Every issue I am addressing here is a call for us to deal with our hearts. How you process the life of your heart will impact everything. For example, the Scriptures contrast a heart that is filled with joy and a heart that is overwhelmed by unhealed sorrow.

> *A joyful heart makes a cheerful face, but when the heart is sad, the spirit is broken.*
> Proverbs 15:13 (NASB)

Look around your community. Go past the surface and take a look into people's eyes. Do you see joy and fulfillment? Or are we witnessing mass numbers of sorrow-filled hearts?

When the heart is healthy, tremendous physical health and wholeness will result. When the heart is filled with sorrow that is not healed or resolved, our spirituality can lose strength. Most people manifest it through sluggishness, weariness or passivity.

Others suppress their pain in chronic busyness and intense drivenness. It's always important to know that suppressed pain will rise up somehow. The negative effects on the heart will trickle down to every aspect of our life.

At the same time, when our heart experiences the love of God, strength and vitality can flow like a river. Confidence soars. Our hope gains power. Faith works richly. You wake up to the life you were meant to live.

But that vitality is not what is often manifesting. Most of the time, it seems we are drudging through mud every day, hoping to get a break from the laborious lifestyle that covers us.

RECOGNIZING YOUR BROKENNESS

Could it be that we are carrying unhealed areas in our heart that serve to increase pressure, negativity, burden-filled living and discouragement? Have you been ignoring broken areas of your heart with constant busyness or a distracted life?

I'm not saying you are a constant mess. Most people can "function" in many areas of their life, while pushing down pain, emptiness and grief. Anytime these areas get triggered, we run and hide, often diving head-first into another distraction. All to keep us from healing that which needs attention.

When someone has a physical wound, it's easy for most to recognize the need for medical attention, care and recovery. But we often lack radar or awareness for the spiritual and emotional wounds we have.

THE SYMPTOMS OF A BROKEN HEART

Many are experiencing these common symptoms of having a broken heart:

- Mood changes.
- Depression, unhealed discouragement.
- Chronic anxiety, panic attacks.
- Numbing out, relational coldness, not being able to connect to feelings.
- Relational isolation and loneliness.
- Cynicism and constant distrust.
- Vulnerability to addictions.
- Chronic workaholism, busyness and performance-based living.
- Confusion, double mindedness and scattered living.
- Burnout and overstressed living.
- Anger episodes that at times, seem to come out of nowhere.

The list can go on and on.

MOVING PAST DENIAL

Most people do not think they have a broken heart. They shrug their shoulders in denial and brush off any need to address life experiences. We can often say *"the past is the past"* more in a protective form of denial than a fruitful belief.

"The past can really be the past" when we allow God to process the life of our heart in a healthy manner.

Others don't think heart healing is necessary. They can stack Scriptures or cliché statements to cover over any need to deal with their brokenness. Yet it still oozes out into their relationship field.

The problem is that we typically don't deal with brokenness until the garbage hits the fan or a crisis appears. At this point, the crisis is often revealing years of neglect to issues of the broken heart.

QUESTIONS FOR CONSIDERATION:

1. Where in your life do you have "head knowledge" about something, but lack the experience of it in your heart?
2. In what way do you find that you cover over the broken areas of your life? Chronic busyness, defensiveness or using some vice to numb the pain?
3. What is one step you can take today to invite God to become more real to your heart and life?

PRAYER:

Father God, I humble myself before You and give You permission to heal me. Thank You for sending Your Son to save me, not just from hell, but from a life bound by brokenness

Thank You for loving me in my junk and weaknesses. I don't always know how to walk in Your healing, but I invite You to be the Healer in my life, in a real way. Take my pain, my mistakes, my emptiness and heartache. I invite You to bring about real healing and change in my heart.

Allow everything You do in my life to be an encouragement to those around me. Use every place You heal to touch the hearts of others. May they feel safe to walk into a greater healing journey.

In Jesus name I pray, amen.

07:
What is a Broken Heart?

He heals the brokenhearted and binds up their wounds.
Psalms 147:3

Ask me 20 years ago, "What is a broken heart?" and I would have responded, *"It's when you go through a breakup with someone you are dating."* Maybe I would add in *"someone who is visibly crying all the time."*

The truth is, most brokenness is in plain sight. You just have to stop and lean into those around you. As you hear their stories and experiences, you will soon bump into the broken places of their heart.

It's ok. We've all got 'em.

Ask me the same question today, *"What is a broken heart?"* and I will say, *"Look around. It's everywhere."*

How do I know this? Because I was one of those who hid my brokenness and kept it under lock and key. I'm also aware because I now spend my life investing in people's hearts "behind the scenes." I've learned over and again that everyone has layers of brokenness that need patient healing.

The only difference between the brokenness amongst us are those who spend their life hiding it and those who chose to embrace the beauty of a healing journey with God. The good news is that Father God's compassion is endless for those who recognize their need for continual healing and maturity. He has an amazing way of addressing our darkest battles, yet in an empowering way that doesn't leave us feeling shamed. If we could all experience this grace, it would lead us to stop playing games with each other. We could all put our masks down and allow God to move in our midst with His healing love.

So, as we move forward, it would help to understand what brokenness is and how it occurs. Some of these meanings overlap, but here are five areas to consider:

1. WHEN SOMEONE'S ACTIONS HURT YOU

The healing journey can often begin with a simple question, like, *"Who broke your heart?"* For most, you can recall a number of painful experiences, where your heart was pierced in significant ways. If you say you have none, then you are probably in denial or haven't lived long enough yet.

For many, when I ask that question, a look of bewilderment appears on their face. No one ever asked them that question, so they don't know how to respond. Others burst into immediate tears, because an unhealed experience quickly rises to the surface. Others give you a blank stare, because they don't realize their history has broken experiences.

The truth is, life brings with it painful experiences that can derail our potential and stunt our growth. Yet in God's eyes, they can become the biggest places for Him to heal us and use us to heal others. That is, if we are open to the healing process.

The first arena of a broken heart is when someone does something directly to you. Most likely, their unhealed brokenness lashed out at you, as they sought to preserve themselves. It was a physical action or words that were said that deeply wounded your heart.

Maybe you responded with tears or anger. It's common that you suppressed that moment out of survival. You didn't say anything, as you hoped to get away from the experience as soon as possible. Regardless of how you responded, someone's hurtful actions can leave a place of pain in your heart.

Pain is often relative--meaning what hurts you deeply may not be as challenging to someone else. But pain is pain, because we are all on a journey at different stages of how we process life.

I spend a lot of my work helping people to recognize how broken experiences in life can affect them. Not to leave them as victims, but to empower them to face the issues of the heart productively. Many times, we just need permission to address the painful experience of life and give ourselves room to process through it.

GOING BACK TO THE ROOT

Now, let me give you a heads-up so that you are prepared. The broken experiences you have had in life often mirror the pain and brokenness you carry regarding your relationship with Dad and Mom. It always goes back to that foundation, for that is where everything began and the early formations of your heart developed.

The Dad and Mom relationship form the scaffolding on which you build how you see yourself, what a relationship with God should be and how to interact with the world you are born into.

So, here is the straight truth: everyone has dad and mom issues to some degree, so relax and take a deep breath. No one was raised with perfect parents. There is only one who is perfect and that is Father God, who wants to show you what it is like to relate to a perfect Father, by helping you process and heal your imperfect experiences.

It took me some time to maneuver through what parental wounds were and how they impacted the life of my heart. As you keep your heart open to learn, God will show you what you need to address, in a way that is loving and empowering.

2. WHEN LIFE CIRCUMSTANCES CRUSH YOU

Life circumstances can take us by surprise and shock us, but they can also erode slowly and gradually wear us down. We are often shocked when life gets challenging, but God never promised that we'd be exempt from hardship.

Jesus even said, *"In this world you will have trouble. But take heart! I have overcome the world"* (John 16:33 NIV). We often believe the error that God should rescue us from all of life's troubles. Yet our God never said that He would remove us from trials, tribulations and troubling experiences. But He did promise to remain with us through them all. His heart is to teach us how to overcome circumstances that at times can seem insurmountable.

But sometimes you just need some validation that what you experienced was tough. Sometimes we pat each other on the back to kindly say, *"Sorry you experienced that, but get over it."* We don't know how to walk with people in their pain and help them navigate through hard times.

The burden and weight of certain troubles can feel like a thousand pounds crushing your chest. Each one of us has our share of trials that take us on for size.

As I reflect on my personal highlight reel, I know there are a number of life circumstances that could have easily crushed me into a bitter pile of numbness.

- Discovering that my first-born son was on the autism spectrum.
- Going through long seasons of financial hardship that never seemed to end.
- Having to make major job changes temporarily, to help my family survive financially.

- Having untrue rumors spread about me that shut down many ministry doors.

Take a moment to reflect on what you've been through. One of the dominant forces that wants to come in through painful experiences is disappointment. Whether it is losing a job, watching a parent die at a young age or experiencing a major kind of let down, disappointment that is unhealed can lead us into anger and cynicism, but it can also shut down our hearts.

Most of us were not equipped to handle the disappointments in life. I haven't met one person who has not had to face circumstantial challenges that at times can take the wind out of their sails.

Instead of slowing down to process what is happening with God, we can make the mistake of moving on as quickly as possible. That is not always the best response. Sometimes you just need to stop and grieve the pain. In deep disappointment, your relationship with God can become more real than ever.

3. LIFE EXPERIENCES QUENCH THE PASSION

A broken heart can come about through passion and dreams being quenched.

Many people leap out of the starting blocks with a fire so strong, but over time, that flame gets extinguished. I have watched scores of people with a hot fire for God, who took tremendous steps of faith, to only years later, get taken out. The resistance they faced wore out their passion.

How many of you in your journey had hopes, dreams and aspirations that never worked out as planned? You had an initial passion, but the lack of results or open doors sucked the life out of your hunger? It's like turning on a garden hose full blast, but the hose develops a kink in the line. Fairly soon, the water stops flowing. Dreams being quenched is like that small kink in the line. If it is not addressed, it can interfere with the overall flow.

4. WHEN YOUR HEART GETS SHATTERED

The word "broken-hearted," as referenced in Isaiah 61 has a vivid meaning, "to burst." It's like having your emotional and spiritual protection ruptured, leaving your heart broken into pieces. Putting it back together can be incredibly challenging and at times, confusing and overwhelming.

So, what do we do about this? And where do we go to process this out? Most people feel left alone in the pain of being shattered, so they go to whatever they can to just get by. They often shove the pain down as far as they can and just get back to busy living. Why? Because life keeps moving. The world doesn't stop because you have a broken heart.

Many shattered people can still show outward success in business and even ministry. They believe that because they have open doors and great opportunities for achievement, their brokenness is not an issue. So, we end up with a lot of people saying "I'm fine" when deep down, they're not. But at some point, we will all be confronted with a choice: *will we face the pain that shattered our hearts?*

SHATTERED RELATIONSHIPS

I believe the number one sign today of a broken heart is emotional isolation. I've been spending years observing what shattered relationships have done to the hearts of people. These relationship wounds create a sense of separation, where over time, they become conditioned to withdraw and isolate.

Isolation does not mean you are not around people. You could be in a room full of people or work with great coworkers around you and still be emotionally isolated. The enemy uses that ground to expand the separation to greater depths.

When your heart becomes shattered, you lose unity and clarity in who you are. You can become easily double minded, insecure and scattered in your perspectives.

People with broken hearts can have a hard time getting clarity and movement, because they are often unclear as to who they are, what they are even dealing with or how to get free. The shattered nature of their heart keeps them from being able to, in unified movement, make steady progress forward.

5. WHEN YOU ARE EMPTY

We live in a sea of emptiness and emotional voids. But do we recognize this is a major sign that your heart is broken?

Emptiness involves the "woundedness of lack," meaning your brokenness stems from what you should have been given, but did not.

- You should have been loved growing up, but you were neglected.
- You should have heard your father's loving words, but didn't.
- You should have received nurture from your mother, but didn't.
- You should have been equipped to live as an overcoming adult, but weren't.
- You were ignored.

Those areas tear at us, but we often don't realize it, so the damage takes place silently. The wound of lack can be very difficult to identify, because it involves NOT receiving what you should have. If you live your whole life ignorant to what you should have received, it can be hard to identify what your emptiness is all about.

Millions of people grow up never getting their heart filled, so that emptiness creates a void--a vortex that attracts broken habits and behaviors. These are null attempts to fill the emptiness.

Most addicts have empty voids in their hearts. They don't know how to process love properly, so they only have a dopamine rush as a reference. They are looking to escape pain, but quite often, that pain includes a deep sense of emptiness that doesn't go away.

When I teach on the Father's love, many people become aware of their broken heart, because they realize they should have experienced love, but didn't. We were all made and designed to be loved and have our hearts filled with a healthy love reference.

Wherever love has not been solidified in our lives, brokenness resides.

- You were born to hear the words *I love you.*
- You were born to see love demonstrated.
- You were born to be equipped as an overcomer.

God gives us the model of earthly relationships to understand His nature. But so many of our experiences have been tainted.

We need healing to our broken hearts.

QUESTIONS FOR CONSIDERATION:

1. In what ways do you find people tend to hide their brokenness?
2. Of the five aspects of brokenness described in this chapter, which one sticks out to your story the most?
3. What would it feel like to have complete safety with God and a few people to process broken areas of your life? With no condemnation, guilt or shame?
4. What did you not receive in your heart that you wish you had?
5. What one thing can you do to position your heart for healing?

PRAYER:

Father God, I come to You in Jesus' name, and I thank You that You love me. I ask that You begin to show me where my heart is broken. I want to be more aware of where You seek to heal and empower my heart. Help me to receive Your loving kindness and healing salve.

Give me the courage to face the hurt in my heart. Set me free from the ignorance I may have to the bondage that is in my life.

Renew my heart and fill those empty places with Your love. You are a Father to the fatherless, so I invite You to come and heal my father wounds. Where my mother may have struggled to nurture me, come with Your comfort and balm of healing to bring rest to my heart. I love You Father God, help me to know You as my loving Father. In Jesus' name. Amen.

08:
Knowing What You Need

To preach good tidings to the poor... Isaiah 61:1

God's work has a specific target: those who recognize their need for heart healing and are ready to humble themselves for His healing work. This may seem like a simple statement, but too many live their lives with little awareness for the deeper work of the heart they need.

But in fact, the Gospel that Jesus delivered, which was prophesied by Isaiah, was a Gospel that must be delivered to the "poor."

To preach good tidings to the poor... Isaiah 61:1

To preach the gospel to the poor... Luke 4:18

Now what does that even mean? Who is the poor person here?

POOR IS NOT JUST A FINANCIAL THING

If you think "poor" simply refers to your financial status, then you're missing the fullness of this invitation. This good news from a good God is not just meant for those who are financially broke. It's also not exclusively targeted to those who are so outwardly broken, the homeless or only those in poverty-stricken nations. Certainly, the work of the Kingdom of God is for them. But too often, the rest of humanity distances themselves from admitting their own spiritual poverty.

Recognizing you are poor is not a pauper mindset. It's a posture of humility, where you recognize your divine need for God to work in your heart continually. You recognize that you are no better than anyone around you, as you could easily fall into any ditch of sin they have stumbled into. You are humbly aware of your own brokenness and are in a continual process of healing and restoration.

"Poor" is a person who realizes they need divine help. You are genuinely humble and lowly of heart. You don't put yourself down, you have submitted your heart to Your Creator and you live out of that reality. There is a vulnerability that you are always "under construction." This cultivates an authenticity amongst your relationships, where you display a healthy need for God and for the people He has put in your life. You never become distant from that.

In modern terminology, we associate "poor" exclusively for those who are struggling financially. In fact, we attach so much value on someone's financial status, to the point that we believe that if someone is financially successful, it means God is blessing all their decisions and ways of life. It is our greatest deception. Subconsciously, we think that someone who has financial abundance is doing well. Yet quite often, those who are financially wealthy can also be the most spiritually and emotionally bankrupt. And they can be the last people to recognize it.

That is why Jesus said, *"it is easier for a camel to go through the eye of a needle than for a rich man to enter the kingdom of God"* (Matthew 19:24). Anything is possible with God, but when riches keep you from being connected to your heart's need of healing, you can easily develop a lifestyle of self-reliance, where your wealth deceives you into thinking "I am all set."

Jesus confronted this arrogance to the Laodicean church in the book of Revelation. They didn't see that they were poor and in need, which distanced them from the deeper work of God.

Laodicea mirrors the modern-day church in many ways, as their sophistication, wealth and status led them to a life of self-deception. They became lukewarm and powerless, because their trust was hard-wired to their resources. Jesus called them to repent, saying, *"Because you say, 'I am rich, have become wealthy, and have need of nothing'—and do not know that you are wretched, miserable, poor, blind, and naked."* Revelation 3:17

Their deception led them to think, "I'm good." When in reality, they had no idea they were naked, poor, blind, wretched and miserable. Those are strong words, showing how misguided the church can be in her self-perception.

This is what we are up against today. Our metrics for what it means to be "rich" are thrown off, while we cover up and avoid facing deep brokenness. Jesus was addressing a church that refused to admit or show their brokenness. It is critical that we break out of this lukewarm state and allow our hearts to engage God in the simplicity of loving fellowship.

> *Behold, I stand at the door and knock. If anyone hears My voice and opens the door, I will come in to him and dine with him, and he with Me.*
> Revelation 3:20 (NKJV) 20

Don't hear me wrong. I am not against rich people, being rich or even having great wealth. What I am targeting is this prevailing message that portrays you don't think you need help. You don't have issues. Everyone else is broken but you.

COVER UPS

This is a tough subject in modern society because we are taught to hide our brokenness at all costs. I spend many hours with various people who have a lifetime of hiding and covering over their weak and wounded issues. Some of them become professionals at covering up. They can quote a list of Scriptures and spiritual statements to distance themselves from appearing flawed.

Social media encourages us to display our best and winning side, while hiding the broken, wounded and weak aspects of our life. We seem to show a lot of "winning" while ignoring the parts of our hearts that are naked, poor, blind, wretched and miserable.

The Pharisees did everything they could to cover up their broken hearts and deep needs. It's easy to view their religious culture with a condescending eye. But we too can find ourselves living like "whitewashed sepulchers;" impressing those around us with great outward expressions, but little attention given to what's underneath.

Why do we do everything we can to keep people from seeing our brokenness? Fear. We are just afraid. The problem is that pride joins our fears, keeping us from just admitting what we need and humbling ourselves to receive it.

THE ANGRY REACTION

The religious people got angry at Jesus, when He presented the Gospel that involved healing of the heart (Luke 4:18). Touching their brokenness triggered an angry reaction. It is the same response you can get from religious people today.

It's amazing that in teaching and writing about the love of God and the process of heart healing, so much anger can get stirred up. Are they angry at me? No. They are angry because there is pain underneath. When you touch pain, often the response is a defense of anger.

They got so angry at Jesus, the Bible says they were strategizing on how they could throw him off of a cliff (Luke 4:29). What were they so angry about? He was hitting at the root problem. Their hearts were broken and needed healing and restoration.

BLESSED ARE THE POOR IN SPIRIT

Jesus declared a blessing to those who are "poor in spirit." In fact, the blessing to them was massive, *"for theirs is the Kingdom of heaven."*

All the resources of heaven are available to those who recognize that in and of themselves, they are spiritually bankrupt and in need of help.

I am in no way advocating that living poor in spirit means we should walk around with our shoulders hunched, reject ourselves or dwell in somber pity. Poor in spirit means you are never far away from recognizing your genuine need for God to do a further work in your heart. You are never distant from needing more healing and transformation. You recognize that you are in process, where there is always room to grow. You are sobered to where you've come from and what God has brought you through.

NEVER TOO FAR

Even though God has freed me of so much mental torment that I struggled with for years, I will never forget what it's like to live in that battleground. I don't *want* to forget what I went through, because it keeps me grounded as I work with others. I guard a sense of sobriety in my heart about it, which keeps me wired to gratitude and my awareness for God's help over my heart.

So, when I sit down with someone who has depression and can't shake it, or I am consulting with a person who has been struggling with anxiety for years and nothing's changing, I don't yell at them to just "get over it." I remember what it's like to be neck deep in those same battles. I know very well what it's like to go through emotional hell and not see the light at the end of the tunnel for a while. Those kinds of experiences humble you to your need and continual need.

I even remember what it was like to deny that I had any issues. I lived like I was invincible. It wasn't until crippling battles came against me, which woke me up to my need. It humbled me like nothing else, calling me to go deeper in my relationship with God.

During that season, I had to bend the knee and humble myself; not just before God, but to those around me. I had to open my heart to become teachable. God even sent people into my life who were not those I would normally hang out with. They were often ministers in the shadows who were keys to my journey. But I had to humble my heart and be ready.

If I can experience these breakthroughs you can too. All it takes is for you to recognize your spiritual and emotional need before God. You will need to let others know this too. Only you can make a decision to become hungry, humble and teachable. With that posture, God can do anything in your life.

A CONDEMNING CONDITIONING

Our condemned and shame-filled self-image keeps us in survival mode. We then waste a lot of time comparing ourselves to others. We look at someone's difficult situation in life and we subconsciously think, *"Well at least I am not that bad."* We are constantly tempted to convince ourselves that we are not spiritually poor and in need.

Many people struggle with being vulnerable and acknowledging their brokenness, because they have been abused by condemnation and accusation from the enemy. They think that dealing with brokenness means they are coming into agreement with an identity of brokenness. They struggle with talking about the past or admitting to weakness, thinking those areas will give the enemy more room to tear them down. This could not be further from the truth.

True vulnerability is an amazing power we carry. In fact, weakness can be our greatest strength. But if condemnation is going to rule our culture, then it's hard to admit to struggles and be open about our deeper need for heart healing.

INVITATION INTO THE PROCESS

I believe that we have made the mistake of describing salvation as a one-time event that solves everything, versus inviting people into a new world, a new identity and new journey. We have developed very weak believers by making the decision of salvation something that solves all their problems, rather than showing that this amazing covenant sets the stage for a beautiful journey of transforming experiences.

I spend a lot of time helping people to lean into the process of growth, maturity, heart healing and transformation. God puts no pressure on you to "arrive" last week. He is so loving and gracious. But life with Him causes us to face our issues and grow. It's just a part of what hanging out with God is like. Yet so many still seek to appear as though they have arrived with no awareness of brokenness and little recognition of weakness.

THERE IS ALWAYS MORE

I am a broken man who is becoming less broken each day. And I am fine with that. I see the eternal destiny that is mine to possess, while recognizing the tension I experience as I learn to come into full agreement with my identity in Christ.

God accepts me. He is willing to grow with me. That does not mean I am less of a believer or less of a person because I have need. It means I'm just honest about my journey. From glory to glory I am being changed.

AWAKENED DISCERNMENT

Here is the "take-home" point in this chapter. The reason understanding your need is so important, is because of the humility it cultivates inside of you. When your heart is teachable and moldable, your self-awareness skyrockets. The heavens open up over your thinking. God truly becomes Lord over your heart. There's less survival games and more freedom to grow in relationship with the Father.

On top of that, your ability to get to the root issues of your heart will happen so much more quickly. Your personal discernment will get enhanced and your ability to see what God is doing in your heart will become so much clearer.

ARE YOU READY?

But you must know, heart healing won't happen until you are ready. God and no other human can force it on you. But there will come a day where all of us have to humble ourselves, acknowledge our need for help and engage the healing our hearts need. It can be a scary step, but also one of the greatest decisions you can make in life.

QUESTIONS FOR CONSIDERATION:

1. Where do you see that people in general avoid their own personal brokenness?
2. What patterns do you find yourself falling into when it comes to your own pain, emptiness and overall brokenness?
3. Do you recognize where you are poor in spirit? How does this impact your heart healing journey?
4. What would it look like in our churches and relationship circles if we all safely shared our struggles together in a loving and productive way?
5. What would help you to take one step into a more authentic heart healing journey?

PRAYER:

Father God, I humble myself before You and admit that I am poor in spirit. I recognize that I am not always open to the heart healing that You have for me. There are times I am afraid of it, too guarded to receive it or too self-righteous to admit that I even have any brokenness. I ask You today to meet me where I am and help me to experience You in a greater depth.

I want to know what it means to experience Your grace and love in a deeper way. Help me to recognize my personal need for continued healing in my life. I renounce any walls that keep me from becoming vulnerable and allowing You to work mightily in my life. Help me to experience a greater depth of You in my heart and life. I look forward to a new and empowered journey. In Jesus name I pray, amen.

09:
Awakened to the Battle

Be sober, be vigilant; because your adversary the devil walks about like a roaring lion, seeking whom he may devour. 1 Peter 5:8

The thief does not come except to steal, and to kill, and to destroy. I have come that they may have life, and that they may have it more abundantly. John 10:10

So, here's the straight-up truth. We are people on a healing journey, immersed in a broken world, where war surrounds us. The pathway you are walking is not a yellow brick road. It's a war path with all manner of tactical ammunition being sent your way.

But it's not the kind of war you may be thinking of. The battle that wages is not person against person. Nor is it a war against yourself, as many are led believe. The battle is with an enemy that seeks to prevent you from a healed and free life. If you are not careful, you can easily fall asleep at the wheel and forget all about the battle you are immersed into.

For we do not wrestle against flesh and blood, but against principalities, against powers, against the rulers of the darkness of this age, against spiritual hosts of wickedness in the heavenly places. Therefore take up the whole armor of God, that you may be able to withstand in the evil day, and having done all, to stand.
Ephesians 6:12-13

You cannot physically see the devil and his army, but you can detect his schemes by what you see manifesting in the lives of people. Furthermore, you can understand his tactics by observing the struggles you face in your own thoughts, the emotions you wrestle with and life events that impact you deeply.

The Apostles carried an awareness of this battle as they *"fought the fight of faith,"* but it often seems the modern church has lost this important narrative. We are therefore left to believe that God has orchestrated all the evil that comes our way, or we beat ourselves up in relentless never-ending self-condemnation and accusation.

Modern civilization often doesn't know what to do with a spiritual warfare grid. Many dismiss it, turning a blind eye to the warfare they face. Others don't know how to apply it in an effective and grounded way.

LOCATING THE BATTLE

The central location of the battle is in your heart. If you listen closely, you can hear it in your mind, but feel it in your heart. The thoughts and impressions you wrestle with reveal what you are up against. Take a moment and consider the feelings you have that are really tough to deal with. Are you aware this is evidence of the battle you are in?

I can easily wake up with a barrage of thoughts that attack before I even know what day it is. Some of it can be due to a bad night of sleep or too many hot wings. But let's get real. You are in a war. It's time you get armed and equipped to fight with greater sobriety.

Notice the resistance that slams against your marriage and parenting. Take a look at the relationship issues that pull the energy right out of you. For many, just getting through the day with peace is a battle in itself.

Observe the feelings and emotions that work against you on a regular basis. Don't assume those thoughts are all your own. In many of them, you are being fed a bowl full of lies, but they are delivered in concealed packages, where the enemy hopes you won't detect them.

AWAKENED TO BATTLE

Jesus won a great victory on the cross and resurrection. Yet there is a war that plays out every day over the lives of people who carry Christ in their hearts. The goal and mission is simple: steal, kill and destroy the God-given potential from your life.

I don't know what you believe about the enemy, but you need to know you have one. You can pretend as though you don't, or theologically push the subject away, but the resistance and tension you face tells you otherwise. That's why the Apostle Peter said, "be sober."

His exhortation is given for a key reason. The state of sobriety is not simply being free from the effects of alcohol, for that is only one aspect of what it entails. Having your sobriety stolen will keep you from seeing the issues of the heart that need to be addressed. Being taken out from sobriety will keep you from seeing the war with full awareness and preparation.

Without sobriety, you will slowly fall asleep, being led into a spiritual coma. The war goes on and you're oblivious to it. Talk to many Christians about their spiritual journey and not much is said about the warfare component. The truth is, they are asleep while the bombs go off, bullets go flying and casualties occur all around. It's one of the reasons why so many hearts are numb and passive. They've tuned out the war and disengaged.

Want to awaken your heart like never before? Come alive to the battle and your role in it.

STEAL, KILL, DESTROY

Jesus said the thief arrives only for three reasons. He's not your friend or ally. He has no other plan, but to steal, kill and destroy.

Our Lord is not being dramatic. You are in the midst of war and you play an intricate part in establishing the power of Christ everywhere you go.

Why is this so important? If you are not aware of the spiritual nature to your battles in life:

- You will become an enemy to yourself, because you will believe that every thought you have originated from your own intelligence.

- You will be tempted to believe that evil coming your way is the result of God orchestrating it.

- You will fail to see what motivates the thoughts and actions of others.

- You will get easily discouraged and worn out, without any vision of what you are up against.

These are just a few. But I cannot emphasize this enough. If you and I are not aware of the battleground we face every day, our hearts don't stand a chance.

Here is where the "steal, kill and destroy" comes against your life:

1. FIND AGREEMENT WITH LIES IN YOUR THINKING.

Most people have not been trained on where thoughts come from, so they assume every thought they hear originated from their own intellect. Without discernment, you can assume all your thoughts are your own, for they arrive in the voice of your own inner dialogue.

This is where we need to sober up the most. Many thoughts you battle with are sent your way by an invisible enemy. The goal is to find agreement in your thinking, so his thoughts become your thoughts. This makes room for more lies to flourish and for the manifestation of those beliefs to become a way of life.

If you are living and breathing, a barrage of destructive thoughts seek to come against you all day, every day. The thief is lurking, searching to find agreements in the most subtle of lies, all to keep you from the conquering destiny that God has invited you into.

THOUGHTS HAVE A SOURCE

All thoughts have a source. You can receive a thought from:

1. Another person communicating to you.
2. God
3. The enemy.

The father of lies is walking about with an army, looking to throw lies at you. But they don't arrive like an external thought. The thoughts of deception from the enemy often sound like your own voice, as though you came up with it completely on your own. Without discernment, you can end up believing that every one of these thoughts originated from your own mind.

When God spoke to Adam about his agreement with sin, the question He asked is, *"Who told you this?"*

> *And He said, "Who told you that you were naked?*
> Genesis 3:11a

One of the first steps towards awakening your heart is to sober up to the thoughts that you wrestle with.

2. CULTIVATE A SENSE OF SEPARATION TO LOVE

Most of the problems you and I face come down to battles surrounding the love of God. If everyone was completely immersed in the Father's love, we'd see a whole lot less of those problems.

That's because God's love is a gamechanger. When you experience that depth of the Father's love, the connection wired to that love is so strong, nothing can stand against it.

That is why there is so much assault over you experiencing the depth of God's love for you. The enemy hopes that at first you will feel separated from God's love, driving you to live a life of performance-based living, where you seek to earn God's love.

Your adversary will also distort what love looks like, so that you stumble through relationships and find yourself locked into habits and coping mechanisms that provide no life. In the end, he seeks to slowly erode the ability for your heart to receive the life of the Father shown through Jesus Christ.

When the Apostle Paul said, *"I am convinced,"* or in other words, *"I am persuaded, that nothing shall separate us from the love of God,"* he was declaring a truth, but one that he needed to come into agreement with. If Paul had to be convinced into this place of conviction, then you and I need to as well.

For I am persuaded that neither death nor life, nor angels nor principalities nor powers, nor things present nor things to come, nor height nor depth, nor any other created thing, shall be able to separate us from the love of God which is in Christ Jesus our Lord.
Romans 8:38-39

3. TRAIN YOU TO THINK YOU ARE YOUR OWN WORST ENEMY

I hear more believers proclaim this lie as though it's their fundamental Christian catechism. They declare, *"I am my own worst enemy!"* as if it was a Scripture verse. Continue to live under this lie and you'll never be able to see yourself as God sees you. The enemy's megaphone will be hidden, as you beat yourself up over all the battles you are having.

God never designed you to be an enemy to yourself. In fact, you are to love yourself as God loves you. But be advised, the assault against you involves making you an enemy to yourself. When this happens, you will look in the mirror with contempt, rather than kindness and empowerment.

4. GET YOU TO FORGET WHO YOU ARE

Identity in Christ is *everything* in the Kingdom of God. You live and flow powerfully from the foundation of knowing who you are. But be advised, your identity is under assault. In every battle that has overtaken me, somehow I lost touch with who God says that I am.

Every temptation of satan against Jesus began with the words, *"If you are the Son of God…"* His deception was seeking to undermine the identity of Jesus. If our Lord was brought into the depths of identity being tested, then know for sure, you will come up against this in your own life.

5. DETERIORATE YOUR RELATIONSHIPS

The easiest way we can see satan's attacks is in the fallout and constant drama in the body of Christ. Nowhere else do our broken-hearted issues come up more, than in how we do relationships.

The division, strife and downright hurt you experience reveal how often the enemy uses broken places in our hearts to erode the quality of relationships. The greatest litmus test of Christian maturity is not rooted in how well you can quote a theological perspective, but in how you are able to do relationships.

6. ACCUSE AND CONDEMN YOU

If you were to imagine your enemy as an army coming against you, the front-line attack is accusation. It's the infantry of satan's work, one that he takes on personally. His name speaks of being an accuser.

No one will live a fruitful life while sitting under thoughts that accuse, condemn and shame. But be advised, it will come against you quite often. In fact, the Bible says the accuser does it day and night (Revelation 12:10). He never rests in seeking to keep you under condemnation.

7. DISCOURAGE YOU AND WEAR YOU OUT

Chinese water torture is a slow, yet systematic drip of water, landing on your forehead that can eventually lead a person to feelings of insanity.

In many ways, the enemy loves to perpetuate destructive thoughts that go on repeat, mostly to wear you out and keep you from prevailing in your battles.

This is why so many of the New Testament letters spoke of living as overcomers, those who take their spiritual battles and allow God to strengthen their long-distance muscles.

In Daniel 7:25, it is said that the saints will come under *persecution*, which speaks of a wearing down, harassment and affliction. In my own life and the lives of those I help, I find the manifestation of this "wearing down" appearing everywhere. Managing our energy and keeping hope alive in our hearts is something that must be daily guarded and watched over. Beware of the spiritual water torture that is slowly stealing the life of your heart.

QUESTIONS FOR CONSIDERATION:

1. When do you find that you can lose awareness that you are in the midst of a spiritual battle?

2. What "agreements" are you becoming more aware of that are disempowering your walk with God?

3. What relationships do you find are under spiritual attack?

4. Where do you find yourself being accused and condemned in your thoughts?

5. When does discouragement and weariness hit you the most?

PRAYER:

Father God, I ask that You awaken my heart to the spiritual battle I am in. May I see the importance of my role as I take on the armor of God into my daily life. Awaken my heart to see who I really am in You and awaken my heart to the power available in You. May my heart be sobered to my assignment, as I learn to overcome.

I ask that You help me to walk with discernment, so that I may recognize the spiritual battle in my thoughts. Help me to not be ignorant of satan's devices, but to walk with spiritual authority over the lies that come my way. I choose to take my stand with You. In Jesus name, amen.

10:
The Four Doorways (Part 1)

nor give place to the devil. Ephesians 4:27

In order to empower your stance in the battle, it is important to be illuminated to what you are up against. Rather than wandering aimlessly through your spiritual journey, you can actually have some greater accuracy in how you free your heart of the lies that hold you back.

My goal is to help keep things simple, as spiritual warfare can be presented in such complicated ways. Well-meaning believers are overwhelmed, scared or quite often, left to spiritual calisthenics, where they are busy with a lot of religious activity, but not much fruit.

It sounds simple, but the battle all comes down to thoughts. Many destructive and lie-filled thoughts bury deep within our heart unrecognized. They influence our belief systems and perspectives, so it's important to become more aware of thoughts the enemy has been sending our way, discern them and remove their influence from our lives.

In order to walk free, it is important to become aware of how the enemy gets destructive thoughts into our hearts in the first place. We can call these "access points" and there are four of them to understand so you can awaken to freedom.

ACCESS POINT #1: INHERITANCE

Many of the thought patterns that you battle have been inherited. In fact, the most challenging thoughts you struggle with are the ones that have been running in your generations for a long time.

Science is confirming this reality, as research is showing that even specific thoughts can be inherited on a genetic level. In my personal work with scores of people, the thoughts they struggle with the most are often carbon copy to what one or both of their parents battled.

Even a casual observation of our genetic heritage can give us a great deal of insight into many of our spiritual battles. If you can, look at your family tree and take notice of patterns that people fell into. Many of those mindsets and struggles will seek to creep up in your own life.

THE FAMILY STRUGGLE

Even though we attempt through human strength to avoid the negative patterns of our family, we can find ourselves struggling with the very same issues, often manifesting at the same time period generations before us did. Those who push extra hard to avoid these family patterns often find themselves in opposite ditches. For example, the child raised with legalistic parents can swing into the danger of lawless and unbridled living.

When you inherit a family thought pattern that is not of God, you become more vulnerable to listening to it. The reason these temptations are more troublesome is because you are not the first recipient. These particular strongholds have been in the family for generations and are now taking you on for size. The mission for these inherited patterns is to build momentum for a worsening effect in your current generation. It's the enemy's way of pushing a growing snowball down the hill.

Some would say we carry the sinful traits of our family because we learned them. Although there is truth to this, there are many hidden battles that are never taught or even brought to discussion in the family, yet they run rampant through the lineage. We also need to consider that adopted children often mirror the battles of the biological parents they never grew up with. Secret battles and hidden pasts tend to repeat themselves, even though they are kept under the carpet.

Medicine and science know that diseases run in families. This is why they examine our family history when doing check-ups or physicals. Personality traits run in families as well. Patterns of anger, fear and addictions can be inherited in generations. Vulnerabilities to certain mental illnesses can travel down the genetic lineage. Patterns of lying or propensities towards sexual dysfunction can run in the family tree as well.

REMOVE OR REPEAT THE PATTERN?

As a part of our healing and freedom journey, we will each have to face those areas that run in our families with a new resolve to overcome. This cannot be done in bitterness, but with a heart to see healing and restoration. Grace must be seasoned on this strategy.

The good news is that God has given us tools to help defeat these inherited battles, the greatest being the gift of repentance. You do not have to serve the sin patterns of your generations. But be aware that some of the thinking patterns will pitch a fit, as they have been wreaking havoc for generations before you.

It is important that we also not approach this subject as victims-- that you are a certain way because of your family line and therefore, you cannot change. This is also not a license to blame and release judgment upon parents and our family trees. This is an opportunity for proper recognition, so that we can take our personal victory seriously, and release spiritual blessing for generations to come.

ACCESS POINT #2: TRAUMA

The heart healing journey is unproductive unless we become aware of the effects that past experiences can have on our present. This especially rings true in the arena of traumatic experiences. The poison and pain coming out of trauma will affect us whether it is expressed outwardly or resides underneath.

I am not a believer of teaching people to obsess about their past with a constant rear view mirror approach--looking back in obsessive introspection. I am, however, completely opposed to living in denial, where we shove down our past experiences without healing.

Healing of a traumatic experience does not begin with ignoring or suppressing what happened, even though many are tempted to do that. The experience needs processing, with safe people and steps that help bring resolution, leading the heart into greater truth and recovery.

Everyone has had various kinds of traumatic experiences. It can be as severe as being involved in military combat or experiencing physical abuse. Or it can be as simple as being left alone, yelled at or accused wrongly in a staff meeting. Here are some more examples:

EXAMPLES OF TRAUMA

- Accidents/Injuries
- Sudden sickness
- Abuse (Physical, Emotional, Sexual or Verbal)
- Spiritual abuse in a church or ministry environment.
- Being neglected or ignored at important moments of need.
- Major moves or transitions.
- Witnessing violence or harm to yourself or someone else.
- Sudden betrayals.

- Being shamed, humiliated or shut out.
- Witnessing harm
- Harsh words
- Being made fun of or bullied.
- Being fired suddenly.
- Sudden financial loss.
- Near drowning or choking.
- Being cheated on.
- Traumatic birth experience.
- Sudden death of a parent.
- Parent leaving suddenly.
- Family crisis

THE IMPACT OF TRAUMA

A trauma is a life event where a person is on the receiving end of a sudden experience that is distressing or disturbing. How traumatic moments effect each person is different, depending on a person's constitution leading up to the event.

The reason a traumatic event has so much impact is because:

1. The event is so unexpected. Your whole system is put under tremendous shock.
2. You are "out of control" to a certain extent. You are not able to compose your thoughts, as the event or series of events often happen so quickly.
3. Your senses are overwhelmed, so you often feel like a pinball machine that has gone "tilt." Your response and reactions are limited.
4. The imprint of the event can travel deep into your memory recall and your physiology.

5. Traumatic events can repeat in a person's life, keeping them stuck in self-sabotaging beliefs, like, *"Men always hurt me. I am accident prone. I am worthless. No one loves me. Everyone takes advantage of me. I am never safe."*

Trauma is a moment in history where the enemy can gain leverage in perpetuating destructive thoughts and lies. Unhealed traumas can often give the enemy a bigger megaphone. This can make moving forward for many, very challenging.

Traumatic moments in life, to any degree, can cause us to pull back relationally and even isolate. We become trained to be apprehensive, hypersensitive and less likely to take risks. The imprint of the pain imbeds itself into the cells of our biology.

In the invisible war of our lives, the enemy looks to apprehend our thinking through traumatic moments, to keep us bound to the replay of the event with little healing. The deepest influence of his deceptive thoughts can find their way through a traumatic experience. In addition, the enemy's desire is to leave you with a disempowering interpretation of the event, leaving you hopeless.

Traumatic moments can be the place where the enemy furthers his work to steal, kill and destroy. Yet they can also become defining moments in our lives, where we can take the pain we have experienced and allow God to heal us in dynamic ways.

QUESTIONS FOR CONSIDERATION:

1. Can you recognize destructive, unhealthy or dysfunctional patterns that run in your family?

2. In looking at your family tree, which patterns do you see manifesting in your own life?

3. Are there any traumatic moments in life that have had a negative impact on your heart? If so, how do you feel it has impacted your life and how you do relationships?

PRAYER:

Father God, I thank You for being a perfect Father and for gifting me with a new inheritance. I come before You and ask that you reveal the patterns in my generations that can be broken by the power of your Son, Jesus Christ. Help me not to become overwhelmed, but to focus solely on what You are showing me.

I thank You that I can live as an overcomer. I do not have to serve the sins of my family, nor do I need to be a carbon copy of the iniquities that my family tree has manifested. Help me to establish a new spiritual lineage for generations to come.

I thank You Father that You are a safe Dad to process pain with. No matter what I have been through, I know that I can safely work through the traumas and painful experiences of life that have pierced me and left me wounded. I know You can take anything in my journey, heal it and show your glory through my heart being changed. So, I invite you to walk with me through these painful areas and lead me into places of peace and recovery. In Jesus name I pray, amen.

11:
The Four Doorways (Part 2)

for we are not ignorant of his devices. 2 Corinthians 2:11b

My prayer is that in becoming more aware of your thoughts, you can develop stronger self-awareness and discernment. So, as you fight the battles you come up against, you don't feel as though you are aimless in your spiritual heart journey.

It can be very freeing to realize that all thoughts are not your own. Separating out the destructive thoughts that you battle against can be a helpful step in experiencing freedom. Identifying access points can also help you learn to gain victory in strategic ways.

ACCESS POINT #3: AGREEMENT

You don't need to have a significant trauma or generations of toxic thinking for the enemy to develop strongholds in your life. All he needs is agreement, where a thought is sent your way, which finds a place of allowance in your own thoughts and beliefs.

Agreements shape your entire life, both the ones you talk about, as well as the hidden agreements that lie underground. Agreements can empower you or disempower you. In fact, everything in our life comes down to the agreements we carry. They form how we think, perceive and view all of life.

Over time, we can become glued to destructive agreements, saying, *"This is just the way I feel"* or *"That's just how I think,"* or the classic, *"This is just the way that I am."* Yet if we were to examine the trail of thought, it would lead us back to the tempter and his army, who are working around the clock to keep us bound to toxic agreements. Your responsibility is to watch over the agreements you carry, casting down any imagination or argument that does not line up with what God says about you.

casting down arguments and every high thing that exalts itself against the knowledge of God, bringing every thought into captivity to the obedience of Christ
2 Corinthians 10:5

Many align themselves with deceptive thoughts as a way of life without any discernment. For some, they can hear a toxic thought and feel as though they came up with it on their own. Others cave into the feelings that arrive with the thought, believing they cannot escape the strong impulses. The less we realize the enemy is speaking, the more dangerous his operations become.

RECOGNIZING THE AGREEMENT

What is an agreement? It's a way of thinking, believing and perceiving that influences how you do life. They are often subtle, yet very influential. If you identify the troubling emotions and limiting perspectives you carry, you will find some form of agreement that is holding it in place.

Agreement is not necessarily something where we consciously say, *"I agree with that."* Agreement primarily comes through tolerating and allowing destructive thoughts and patterns to accumulate within. If we struggle with fear, then we have agreement with fear in our thinking. If we battle with being easily resentful, then we are in agreement with bitterness and resentment. If speaking ill about people behind their backs is a constant habit, then we have agreement with accusation and gossip. Walking into a room and believing, *"No one loves me,"* gives room for agreement with rejection.

Thoughts from the enemy are presented to us in a medley of forms. Everything from feelings, impressions, reasonings, temptations and false beliefs, all with audio and video playback included, can originate from the enemy's camp. Most people entertain whatever comes down the pike in their thoughts without awareness.

Spiritual warfare is often simpler than we make it. Where there is agreement, the enemy has access. We cannot make it so complex that we lose this simple truth. Satan is the ringleader and father of all lies that go against the knowledge of God.

The first example of agreement is revealed in the garden with Adam and Eve. Satan presented an initial thought that was loaded with deception, but was presented in a way that would lure them in. The devil was seeking for agreement, knowing it would produce a destructive action.

Once his lies found a landing place in their own thoughts, Adam and Eve acted on the deception, eating the fruit they were told not to eat. With Adam's agreement and subsequent actions, an additional flood of thoughts and impressions, including fear, uncleanness, guilt and shame, came upon them.

This drove them to hide from God. As God approached Adam, His response revealed the intrusion of deception into their thoughts, as He said, *"Who told you that you were naked?"* In other words, God was saying, *"Who are you agreeing with in that thought?"* (See Genesis 3)

WALKING OUT OF AGREEMENT

Please understand that because we are presented with a thought does not mean we are "one" with that thought immediately. Most of the toxic thinking that flies across the screen is just a form of temptation. Having a thought simply means that we are presented with an opportunity for agreement.

For many, certain thoughts have been so familiar that agreement goes on without any awareness. They fly right past temptation and into agreement instantly. It has now become a way of life for them.

The good news is that we do not have to agree with the enemy's thoughts anymore. In fact, as we remove counterfeit ways of thinking, we have a great opportunity to become filled with how God thinks, immersed with His life, love, truth and power!

What breaks agreement with the enemy is *repentance*, a word which speaks of moving from one way of thinking and into another. Repentance shuts off all four enemy access points. It also turns our hearts to welcome the mindset of God to lead our lives.

The repentance that removes agreement is not always a one-time event. It's often a developing process, where we learn to turn from ways of thinking that have become weeds, while planting the seeds of God's thoughts into the soil of our hearts. This takes time, but making the initial decision to break agreement gets the process moving into an empowered direction.

ACCESS POINT #4: A BROKEN HEART

Your enemy has a mission to steal, kill and destroy through places of unhealed brokenness in your heart. This is where the war wages intensely, because most sin on this planet manifests out of broken issues of the heart that have not been healed by God. Your most intense battles of the heart and mind often stem from those broken places that need the healing touch of the Father.

Your heart collects the experiences of life, which then get funneled into how you think and believe. How you walk through these experiences will determine what the life of your heart will manifest.

The Bible shows us how pain of the heart can impact our spirituality.

A merry heart makes a cheerful countenance: but by sorrow of the heart the spirit is broken.
Proverbs 15:13 (KJV)

Having a heart filled with joy is not only healthy to the body, but it gives an outward expression of God's love for the world to receive. Have you ever noticed there is so much you can see in someone's life by looking at their countenance? We are often wearing the disappointment, pain and hurt of our hearts.

When the heart is truly healthy, the whole person is healthy. Even when sorrow enters, a healthy heart knows how to process through the pain, allowing God to bring healing to the broken issues of life.

We all face experiences that create sorrow in our heart. This is normal and a part of life. What is unhealthy is when the sorrow is never addressed and brought into a healthy perspective.

I have observed scores of people who have not allowed the healing work of God to bring past pain into resolution. The person may act like life is fine, but they carry the bondage underneath; coming out of unresolved pain.

Sorrow which does not find proper healing and recovery creates a brokenness in the spirit of a person; leaving them more vulnerable to the enemy's devices. Our ineffectiveness in overcoming the enemy is often connected to not addressing the wounded heart properly. So, a good question we may need to ask ourselves in uncovering enemy access is, *"Where is my heart broken?"*

Whether you've had an amazing upbringing or not, we all have forms of brokenness that we carry. So, here is a tip for your heart healing journey: there will be many opportunities in life for you to address the broken issues of your heart. Be open to realizing that many of the battles you face will reveal broken areas of your heart that need healing and maturing. You may think it's about other people or circumstances needing to change, but I find that God will use these challenging seasons of our lives to awaken us to our need for Him to heal us in deeper ways.

QUESTIONS FOR CONSIDERATION

1. In looking over your journey and battles, in what areas of your life has there been agreement with the enemy's thoughts, impressions and temptations? Write them down.

2. Have you considered that your heart may be broken? In what ways do you find that brokenness manifests in your life?

PRAYER

Father, I submit my heart to You and I ask that You examine me. You know me better than anyone. I submit the areas that I am battling and I trust You to show me where I need more freedom. I pray that You help me to understand what is hindering and keeping me from a whole relationship with You and others.

Help me to have discernment of my battles. Give me the courage to face them and shut the door to the enemy's access. I pray You teach me to be awake where I have been in denial. I thank You that You will love me the whole way through this.

Help me to see the agreements in my life that are hindering my journey and keeping me from all that can be experienced in You. I pray this all in Jesus name, amen.

12:
The Wounds We All Carry

When my father and my mother forsake me, then the Lord will take care of me.
Psalms 27:10

The hurt and pain of life will collect inside our hearts, no matter how much we try to push it away. In today's fast-paced culture, it's easy to move on to the next event in life without realizing how broken experiences have piled up. A large percentage of people saunter on while carrying an unhealed accumulation of hurt in their hearts.

We live with this because people typically underestimate how things have impacted them and they overestimate how quickly they should dust off every negative experience. Many appear to live well by this lifestyle, but the unaddressed pain of the heart will manifest in some form or fashion down the road.

I've witnessed this far too many times. At certain occasions I would say to myself, *"Well, maybe it's just me. That person is probably just stronger than I am."* And yet years later I would hear of them having an affair, a nervous breakdown, sex addiction or some form of mental health issue. Much of this was due to neglecting the wounds of the heart.

TWO KINDS OF WOUNDS

As you delve into heart healing, I want to make you aware of two main wounds, the second of which can be harder to detect.

The first involves wounds of hurt, things that directly happened to you; negative experiences which impacted your heart, whether you are aware of it in the moment or not. It does not matter how many times you yell, *"I am bulletproof!"* Negative experiences have an impact on your life to some degree.

I'm not saying that everything that happens to you should send you running into an emotional emergency room. But I do want to encourage you to be aware that you have wounds that influence your thinking and behavior.

These wounds may lead back to abusive experiences, hurtful words or slander against you. Betrayal is one of the most painful relational traumas people experience. Some of the great men of God in the Scriptures, including King David and Jesus Himself experienced the harsh pain of relational betrayal. Whenever you experience this form of woundedness, what was done to you leaves a gash in your heart that needs attention.

The second kind of wound is much harder to detect at times. This is the wound of lack. For most people, it lurks underneath the surface. This type of wound involves the experiences you *should* have had, but didn't. It involves an aspect in life where somebody should have loved you, but didn't. They either didn't have it to give or they were so focused on themselves, they left you in an unloving situation.

HEALING HUMAN EXPERIENCES

The reason why it's important to address the unhealthy human experiences we've had, is because these wounds infect how we view God and how we process relationships. Your earthly grid of experiences have a high level of influence upon your spiritual perspective and vision for the future.

Earthly relationships are meant to give us references in relating to God. For example, God calls Himself a Father. Therefore, we will relate to God in many ways through the lens of how we relate to our earthly father. He carries the mold for our "God-lens."

So, for you, what comes to mind when you hear the word "father?" Or "Dad?"

Let's also talk about our mothers. Your ability to receive nurture from the Holy Spirit has connections to how well your mother was able to nurture you growing up.

So, what was your relationship with your mother like? Was it a healthy one?

Jesus is called our elder Brother, a reference leading us to a safe and empowering older sibling, who cares for us and looks out for us. A healthy older brother sticks up for you and shows you how to relate to the father.

So, what is your reference? When I mention "brother," do you feel loved and protected?

What about family? The Bible calls believers the family of God, but the mere thought of family or family gatherings can induce painful memories. More families than not have created deep damage in the lives of its members. So, chanting out, *"we are the family of God!"* actually needs a renewed perspective of what healthy family should even look like.

I could go on and on with other references, like how marriage is meant to teach us about our relationship to Jesus. The point of all this is simple: earthly relationships, though flawed, were meant to give us tangible references in relating to God and the body of Christ. The truth is, these references have been deeply damaged and need healing.

You and I have wounds of hurt and wounds of lack from both male and female interactions. Most of the time, we can get locked up in the present relationship frustrations or hurts. But we don't realize that the present relationship is not the issue. Tell me about any struggle in your life, there is often a cord that leads back to your first relationship reference--dad and mom; the core place in your heart that God needs to heal.

GETTING TO THE ROOT OF HEALING

As you move yourself towards the root system of heart healing, there are some important questions you'll need to address. They may be challenging to consider, yet they reveal the core issues that need tending to.

The first question is, *"What was your relationship with your earthly father like?"* The more you can answer this honestly, the better you can address what your heart needs.

Here are some further questions:

- *Was he a spiritual leader in your home?*
- *Did he express his love for you in his words and actions?*
- *Was he easily accessible when you needed him?*
- *Was he a safe place of love?*

Most of all, did your father *equip* you to enter the world as an overcoming adult? All effective parenting is meant to transition you into adulthood with tools to face life effectively. The father is meant to be the leading source of equipping in this area.

All healing of the heart begins with healing the father wound. He is the one who was meant to establish love, identity and self-esteem in your life. His job is to set the grid of love in your heart so that you can relate to Father God in a healthy way and enter the world as an overcomer.

The majority of problems in society stem back to the lack of a father's love and investment in a child's life. Most grow up without a healthy compass for love and identity, with little tools to overcome, stemming back to what they did not receive from their father.

The truth is, most dad's struggle to be a powerful presence in the home because they were never given it themselves to begin with. They only gave out what they received. When it comes to loving and equipping his children, most dads don't know what to do. Therefore, he often immerses himself in his work. Many fathers bail on the family completely. Most live very emotionally and spiritually passive, leaving the mother to carry a heavy load in the home.

A large percentage of moms are left with most of the leadership burden in the household. Because of this, she is often exhausted, angry and even depressed. In the midst of this leadership absence, she takes on more than she was ever meant to. The mom will either become so distracted by her unhealed brokenness or she will stuff it all down and soldier on. Therefore, the children are not able to receive the full amount of nurture from her they were meant to.

HEALING THE MOTHER WOUND

This leads us to the second important question. *"What was your relationship like with your mother?"*

This question can be the trickiest. Addressing mother issues can feel dishonoring or disrespectful, especially because most mother's carry an excessive spiritual and emotional burden in the home. But the wounds we carry are present, nonetheless.

Further questions can help you process healing:

- *Was your mother a safe source of nurture in your life, teaching you how to process pain and recover from emotional challenges?*
- *Did she love you when you needed it?*
- *Was she emotionally available to you?*
- *Did she comfort you in times of struggle?*

Furthermore, did your mother equip you with a capacity for nurture and emotional health? Were you able to move into adulthood with an ability to regulate your emotions and engage relationships in an effective way?

The power of a healthy mother relationship will impart a well-rounded reference for nurture, which is how we develop emotional and relational health. Nurture welcomes people into safe and comforting relationships, which is what a healthy mother provides.

Nurture is also developed in how you receive affection growing up. Your relationship with your mother will greatly impact how you are able to give and receive affection. Through hugs, kisses and comforting words, those affectionate experiences build a healthy familiarity with the power of God's nurturing love.

God is our Heavenly Father, but he also intended for His nurture to be seen through the lives of healthy mothers. You learn nurture from both your dad and mom, but the mother provides nurture in a way that is all her own. With nurture properly established, both men and women can grow up with emotional stability and a healthy ability to love themselves.

The mother wound is one that takes time to understand. Most do not see it at first. But a growing percentage of people carry unaddressed mom wounds, simply because their mother could not or would not nurture them in the way they needed.

Perhaps mom left. Or maybe she was physically present, but emotionally absent and detached. It's possible she was preoccupied with being angry at your father. Many moms never received affection from their own mothers, so her empty heart left her to become an emotionally cold mother.

HEALING AND CHANGING THE GENERATIONS

It is so important to recognize the impact of our father and mother relationships. Otherwise, we can carry unhealed wounds into our present and future relationships. We will end up repeating the patterns in our generations, until someone has the courage to receive the healing that is needed.

So, where do you begin? Here are some practical ways to allow healing to open up:

1. Recognize the wounds.

All healing begins with recognition. This is not a license to blame your parents or dishonor who they are. Rather, it is an opportunity for simple recognition. There's no shame in realizing what you came from or recognizing the negative experiences you've had.

Take your time. Do not rush this process. Remember, you are on a journey, not a quick-fix track. You may need to find a mentor or safe person to process some of these wounds, so you can get some healthy input.

2. Open your heart to receiving God's love.

To receive God's love, you need to know who He is as a Good Father. Your references will need to be renewed. Sometimes an honest and humble prayer can help the process tremendously.

I remember one day saying, *"God, I do not know you as a Father or a Dad. I don't know what it's like to receive Your love. But would You show me?"*

This prayer positioned my heart to learning what a good father is and learning to receive that great love.

3. Forgive your parents for not being what you needed.

Every parent has their share of flaws and shortcomings. Those wounds of hurt or wounds of lack need to be forgiven. Otherwise, those pains will have permission to stick with you and steal your peace. Furthermore, the sins they brought against you can be easily repeated in your life unless forgiveness is processed out.

When we embrace the forgiving heart of God, we learn to see people and ourselves in a whole new way. Our lens gets cleared up and we engage relationships in a more empowered way.

If you feel that forgiving your parents seems nearly impossible, start by making a decision to head that way. If you don't *want* to forgive, then God's healing work won't happen. But God will work powerfully with a heart that *wants* to forgive. The choice of where you are headed is up to you.

4. Learn what it means to live as a loved child of God.

Your brokenness will form how you see yourself. Many of us sought for the love and affection of our parents, but did not receive it. Therefore, we took on some role as a way to earn their love and approval. It may have been a performer, achiever, problem solver, perfectionist or many other roles that became unhealthy burdens you took on.

Part of your healing process will involve letting go of that broken role as your core identity. Any identity that is not based on being a loved son or daughter of God is a counterfeit.

You may have many roles in life, but those roles are not who you are. Who you are is not based on what you do. Your core identity is a loved son or daughter of God.

It is time to get to know who you really are. Even though you may be a grown adult, God wants to restore the simplicity of knowing what it means to be His loved child. It's time to stop a life of only *doing* . . . and focus your heart on BEING.

QUESTIONS FOR CONSIDERATION:

1. In reviewing the influence of father wounds, what wounds do you carry from your relationship with your earthly father?
2. In what areas do you wish your father equipped you more?
3. Did you miss out on your mother's nurture?
4. What did you long for from your mother relationship that you did not receive?

NEXT STEPS & RECOMMENDED RESOURCES

Online Videos and Prayers:

Go to markdejesus.com/thhjoc for video insights and healing prayers for your heart healing journey.

Recommended Resources:

The following additional recommended resources can be found at markdejesus.com.

Experiencing God's Love as Your Father (Book and Online Course)

Exposing the Rejection Mindset (Book and Online Course)

13:
The Power of Self-Acceptance

But God demonstrates His own love toward us, in that while we were still sinners, Christ died for us.
Romans 5:8

Quite often, I find myself meeting with someone who is desperate for help, but emotionally spent over what they are going through. As they share the battleground, thoughts feel like spaghetti and emotions are fried to the point of numbness. Frustration is so pent up, they are about to explode. As they share their story, a tension rises in their voice.

A personal hostility swells within them. The reality is they are angry with themselves. They can't seem to find a way into freedom and therefore, they are filled with disgust over their lack of progress. A driving thought comes to the surface, saying, *"why am I still struggling?"*

The pain goes even further to ask, *"What is wrong with me? I shouldn't have these problems! I should be over this by now! Why can't I get it together?"*

After a complete dump of verbal frustration, they immediately start backpedaling, apologizing for expressing so much negativity.

With overtones of religious condemnation, they say, *"I know I should be better than this."*

As this person gives me room to share my input, my reply often surprises them. What I have to say is simple, yet incredibly powerful, speaking to what they really need in the midst of their battle.

"It's ok that you are not ok."

Some are shocked by this. They are used to receiving the shameful disappointment of others, who wonder why they can't just get over it. They are also used to hearing about the next three steps they should apply, or a packet of to-do lists they will never be able to fulfill.

In the midst of this, many never consider the power of God's love to first accept them, right where they are in their junk.

We're taught the power of God's loving acceptance at salvation, but somehow, we lose sight of it for the rest of the journey. Yet this precept cannot be skipped over. The first experience for healing of the heart involves experiencing the complete and unconditional acceptance of God's love.

Unless this environment is set in your heart, you will waste your life trying to heal and change with cycles of self-help steps. The power of love will be missing from your life and you will struggle with a lifetime of self-pressure and frustrated living. Before you take any healing steps, you must learn to engage self-compassion and lovingly accept yourself, right where you are.

ENGAGING SELF-COMPASSION

When you look at yourself and say, *"It's ok that I am not ok,"* you allow your heart to engage the first fruit of God's love. His love accepts you, right where you are. God does not change your problem and then love you. He loves you endlessly from the beginning and forevermore. He approaches every struggle and battle you have with a compassionate acceptance that will fuel you into breakthrough.

Self-compassion and the acceptance of love does not leave you unchanged. It sets the atmosphere by which God's power works. You cannot experience long-term transformation without first experiencing the atmosphere of God's loving acceptance. He doesn't ignore sin, but He also doesn't withhold love until you have conquered sin. He loves you first, right now, in the midst of your mess. In fact, He will love you even if you never decide to change.

Many seek transformation but skip this stage. They often avoid it because it will lead them to confront the anger and self-hatred they have towards themselves. Most people cannot receive love, until they feel they get to a point where they are "worth" being loved.

Others would say if we truly let ourselves engage the power of self-acceptance, then we will not change and even tolerate sinful lifestyles. This is a limited view of love. If love accepts you right where you are, but provides no avenue of hope for change and transformation, then it's not really true love.

You cannot move into the greater depths that God's love has to offer unless you immerse yourself in understanding how He sees you in your sin and struggles.

MY STRUGGLE WITH SELF-ACCEPTANCE

I lived my whole life with a deep passion for growth and transformation. But there were many struggles I could not shake off right away. Some never seemed to stop. The more I tried, the worse it got at times.

I carried a deep anger, continually beating myself up for the lack of progress I seemed to be manifesting. Meanwhile, I was relentlessly hard on myself in how I evaluated my journey.

After years of living like this, the frustration led me to face myself in a whole new way. I wanted results, but I did not love myself. God entered into my pain to teach me how to see myself with new eyes.

I didn't know how to be ok with not being ok. In my conditioning, it was unacceptable. It felt like failure. So, for most of my life, I built a foundation on making sure I was "good" for people. I didn't know how to make room for weakness, mistakes and struggle, without feeling deep shame and embarrassment.

I felt like when I wasn't "good," a giant spotlight was on me, as if everyone was gasping at the sight of, *"Mark's not doing good!"* I always felt I had to be strong for everyone. So, when I was not, I didn't know how to manifest it in a healthy way.

When I learned to experience self-compassion, God's love became more real to me. This loving acceptance gave me a powerful glimpse of the Father's perspective over my life and battles. It also became a major turning point for growth and empowered decisions. I was able to see life with greater clarity. Love gave me that ability.

THE NEED FOR LOVE OVER YOUR SITUATION

The power of God's love arrives to meet us in our condition. The Scriptures say, *"Love covers a multitude of sins"* (1 Peter 4:8 NIV). Love does not hide sin to pretend it's not there. Love creates the atmosphere by which sin can be addressed in the most powerful way.

Without love, all you see is guilt, condemnation, shame and judgment. You are left staring at the size of the problem while losing sight of the solution. With love, you are invited into redemption and transformation. The atmosphere is set for the freedom from sin to be experienced.

Love welcomes the grace of God to work powerfully, no matter what your current state is. God loves you, not because you are doing well. He loves you because He loves you. But many are struggling to receive it and give it to themselves. They may want change or breakthrough with all their might, but they keep skipping past their need to experience self-acceptance.

LOVE FIRST

Practicing self-acceptance does not work when you arrive at some level of achievement. You need it right now. It starts right now. Love does its best in moments where it seems you don't deserve it, or you struggle to receive it.

Saying to yourself, *"It's ok that I am not ok"* will send shockwaves against all the strongholds of self-hatred, performance pressures, perfectionism and those battles you have with yourself.

At first, many receive this exhortation with open arms. But they later come back to me and say, *"I 'accepted' myself, but I am just sick of being broken! Now what do I do?"* I understand the frustration, but the hostile intensity is often a sign of being hard on yourself. Anger is rising up. It's a sign that loving acceptance needs to have a deeper work. You don't just flip a switch and everything gets easier. Self-acceptance opens up a whole new pathway that we need to learn to live in. It takes time.

WHAT DOES THIS LOOK LIKE?

In a practical sense, there are some helpful ways you can exercise self-acceptance in the midst of your battles.

1. Accept yourself in your current state.

This can be hard for many die-hard, performance-based Christians. They automatically think acceptance means you don't seek further change. Yet they forget that every day, God accepts us in Christ Jesus, even though each of us have numerous battles that we have not overcome.

Jesus taught that it's easy to love those who are nice to you. In applying this towards yourself, it can be easier to love yourself when life is going well. But when you are struggling, that's when the resistance really shows itself. But this is when love needs to be applied the most.

The first step is to give yourself total unconditional acceptance in your current state. If you beat yourself up and rev up the engines, then the change is all on you. But when you welcome the power of loving self-acceptance, you open your heart for God's grace to take over and lead you into transformation.

2. Look at what you are going through without instant judgment.

So many approach the battle zone of their lives with an intense and militant approach. Though we live in a warfare zone, you cannot deal with yourself as a drone, robot or machine. You are a human who has feelings and thoughts that take time to process through. Although you live in a war, you cannot scream at yourself like a drill sergeant all the time and experience a full life from the heart.

Exercising self-compassion means you look at where you are without instant judgment. Most who are hard on themselves instantly judge their struggle. When it comes to taking thoughts captive, many try to manage their thoughts without the presence of love. They become harshly black and white and legalistic in how they process what they are thinking and feeling. Without love, you will get legalistic and punish yourself within. There's no freedom in that.

Love and grace will free you from legalistic judgment and instead lead you into relational connection. In the context of relationship is where God meets us and transforms our hearts.

The power of self-acceptance will quiet the constant criticisms you have about yourself, where you come under the pressure of chronic evaluation and assessment of all the issues you need to work on. If transformation always exhausts you, love needs to have its deeper work.

If every time you met a friend, they only talked about what was wrong with you, judged you and pointed out all the things you needed to work on, we would say that relationship is abusive. But we tolerate this kind of interaction in our thoughts towards ourselves all the time.

It's time to let love in, so the inner critic can die.

3. Look with the eyes of love.

When you say, *"It's ok that I am not ok,"* you invite God's love to give you eyes to see yourself as He sees you. You take off the lens of anger and condemnation towards yourself and you put on God's eyesight.

For most perfectionists, flaws are seen as unacceptable. Weakness cannot be tolerated. You see mistakes as absolute failure. The war waging inside of you will not let you land into the arms of God's love, accepting you in your current state.

Your first step may need to be a simple prayer that says, *"God, give me the eyes to see myself the way You see me."*

Let His love have a work in your life. The acceptance of love will lead you to the next level of what love offers, which I will address in the next chapter.

QUESTIONS FOR CONSIDERATION:

1. As you say the sentence out loud, *"It is ok that I am not ok,"* do you find it hard to accept that statement?

2. What reasons come up that keep you from landing into greater self-compassion?

3. What current situation are you facing that needs the power of self-acceptance today?

PRAYER:

Father God, I thank You that You accept me with Your eternal love, right now, right where I am. I acknowledge that I struggle at times to receive it. I don't give that compassion to myself and I want to learn how to love myself in the power of Your compassion for me.

I ask that You help me to break through the resistance that rises up, seeking to keep me from loving and accepting myself in my current state. I ask that Your perfect love would lead me to see my life the way You see me. Help me to carry eyes of compassion in how I view myself and my battles.

I thank You Father that You love me and will always love me. In Jesus name I pray, amen.

14:
Your Need for Patience

let patience have its perfect work... James 1:4

One of the predominant questions I get asked by well-meaning people who desire greater transformation is, *"How long does it take to get free?"* Those who ask this are working through a battle they are trying to overcome, but they feel as though progress is taking forever. Depression often sets in. Many long for the future to get better, but they are up against the same struggles that have been around for some time.

That question brings me back to a time where I was battling debilitating anxiety, obsessive thoughts, panic attacks and relational phobias. If ten was the worst, I was at a nine or ten every day for a long time. Twenty-four hours a day, seven days a week, I was drowning.

I sought out for help everywhere I could. Talking to friends, mentors, counselors while devouring books and resources, I dove into any source of help I could find. Now keep in mind, this was during the early 2000s. There were not a lot of available resources online that addressed these mental health subjects. No one in the church was talking about anxiety like I was facing. OCD was only seen as battles that "clean freaks" had.

On top of all this, I was a pastor at the time. The stigma and shame for having these battles was intense. Back then, I felt so overwhelmingly alone in a sea of mental and emotional storms. It seemed almost impossible to possess internal peace.

I slowly began to get understanding on what I was up against and how to walk free. I positioned myself to be as teachable as possible, so I could gain all the insight and tools I could to experience freedom. But I bumped up against a constant discouragement of feeling I was continually looping in the same struggles with no sight of major progress.

THE PIVOTAL MOMENT

I remember one particular day very clearly when I was headed to a social gathering. I was overwhelmed with how many mental and emotional spider webs I was trying to clear out. Discouragement and chronic symptoms of depression were rising. I found I was getting angry with myself, while being tempted to get angry with God. *"When's this going to end? When's the anxiety going to break? When am I going to get free? When are things going to get better? I mean, come on!"*

Have you ever felt this way?

In the midst of this lack of peace, I took a deep breath and cried out to God for clarity. As I'm walking towards the home of this social gathering, I'm having a conversation with myself and God. During this inner dialogue, a thought came to me from 1 John 4:18, which said, *"he who fears has not been made perfect in love."*

A light bulb went off in my mind. *"The reason I am anxious is because love has not been experienced in those areas of my heart."*

This became a major revelation and turning point for my heart transformation.

A LOVE ISSUE

My problem was not an intelligence issue, it was actually a love problem. My symptoms were revealing a love deficit in my life. In fact, the majority of battles we face, reveal the areas where love has not had a deeper work.

In this moment, I became highly aware of my need to grow in what love meant. All of us have areas in our heart where love has been absent or compromised. It often takes a while to realize it.

While my symptoms were incredibly frustrating to deal with, I was awakened to the reality that learning to settle in God's love was a journey, not a light switch. I had some learning to do. I needed to give myself time to learn about love, as well as how to give and receive love with greater freedom. It takes time and there is no way around it.

LEANING ON THE PILLARS OF LOVE

This led me to understanding two main pillars of love that you and I need to experience on a regular basis. As self-acceptance welcomes you into connection with God, the power of love goes further to empower your transformation.

These two pillars are the opening traits of love found in 1 Corinthians 13. One is patience, the other is kindness. The power of what love bestows upon our life settle on these two very important blessings of love.

Kindness is what love gives out. Patience is what love can handle.

This cannot be skipped over. In that moment where I am dwelling on 1 John 4, I realized that what I needed in that moment was patience. My zealous desire to experience freedom had taken over, to the point that it was overriding the voice of God's love. Just as we can skip over self-acceptance, the patience of love can be forgotten in the midst of our desire for healing and change.

LEARNING PATIENCE

In this moment, it dawned on me how incredibly impatient I was with myself and my journey. The pressure of perfectionism and intense expectation overrode the power of God's loving patience with my journey.

To regain the power of patience, I spoke a simple statement over my heart which transformed my trajectory forever. It began to align me with God's love over my journey.

I looked at everything I was battling and firmly said, *"It will take as long as it takes."*

Healing will take as long as it needs to take.

Transformation will take as long as it needs to take.

This one statement began to release the pressure off my life, of feeling as though I needed to be "better" long ago. The yoke of pressure was being traded for the yoke that Jesus offers, which He says is light.

When it comes to transformation, there is no pressure from God for you to hurry up and achieve some state of breakthrough. He is more patient than you could ever imagine. Just when you've received a cup of His merciful patience, you realize there remains an entire ocean of His patience to experience.

But I needed to give this to myself. It is one thing to know God is patient, but I needed to receive it. God's patience does not have its impact if I respond with impatience towards myself.

PATIENCE ENHANCES TRANSFORMATION

Here is the paradox I discovered. When I engaged the power of patience with my whole heart, it actually accelerated my healing and freedom journey. When I lived under self-pressure, it slowed everything down and actually made it harder. Patience actually sped up the trajectory of my transformation.

When I engaged patience and let go of the yoke of pressure, I was able to see the long view, versus focusing on whether or not I was having instant breakthrough. My eyes were open to seeing that I didn't get here overnight. Therefore, I needed to sit back, let the journey open up and take its course.

And by the way, *"It will take as long as it takes."*

LEANING INTO PROCESS

Patience plugs you into the journey and relieves you from "destination disease." Your healing is going to be a process. I'm not going to figure it all out overnight and neither are you. The more room you make for process and the journey, the more effective transformation will become. You and I have to grow in a process that takes time; way more time than we ever anticipated.

The enemy will accuse you and add pressure, telling you that you should have arrived long ago. When you say, *"It will take as long it takes,"* it disempowers the enemy's tactics. It says to the inner critic, *"So what if I've not arrived. I am on my journey."*

CASTING OUT PERFECTIONISM

One of the great enemies to transformation is the toxicity of perfectionism. It robs you of process and conditions you to live under constant pressure, leaving you in a defeated lifestyle.

In God's eyes, His perfecting work flows through His loving patience. James says, *"Let patience have its perfect work, that you may be perfect and complete, lacking nothing."* (James 1:4). That word translated "patience" also speaks of endurance, an ability to steadfastly wait.

You want to experience the greatest amount of transformation, maturity and growth? Learn to immerse yourself in patience. In your heart healing journey, let patience have the work it needs to have.

Is it that simple? Sounds easy, but in the midst of life, being patient is one of the most challenging traits to exemplify. Yet God says His perfecting work is found when we exercise patience.

So, here is what we need to say. In the midst of your most difficult days and struggles to find breakthroughs, it's time to declare:

IT WILL TAKE AS LONG AS IT TAKES.

QUESTIONS FOR CONSIDERATION:

1. Where do you find that your passion for change and transformation can work against you when patience is not involved? In what way does impatience steal the power of your heart healing journey?
2. In what area of your life does patience need to be exercised more?
3. What would it look like to live with greater patience?

PRAYER:

Father God, I am becoming more aware of my need for patience. In my passion for freedom, I can become hard on myself and come under the yoke of pressure. Today, I chose to take on the yoke of Jesus, which is light and without pressure. I make a decision to yield to the power of Your loving patience towards me. I ask that Your patience would land in my heart and transform how I see myself and my journey.

My prayer today is that patience would have a perfecting work in my heart and life. May peace settle in as I let Your love lead me into greater patience. I didn't get here overnight. I recognize that my healing journey will take some time. I chose to let go of the "time-table pressure" and let the journey take its course.

It will take as long as it takes. I release my journey to You, Father. In Jesus name I pray, amen.

15:
What Does Love Say?

Love is patient, love is kind… 1 Corinthians 13:4a

Once and for all, I want to help you drown the inner critic. There is nothing more disempowering to progress than the inner voices that resist you at every turn and leave you feeling defeated. They relay thoughts and feelings that beat you up and keep you bound in your battles.

I believe one of satan's top assignments is to make you an enemy to yourself in your thoughts. When you become a villain against yourself, the inner critic becomes a dominant voice in your life. Most people become "one" with the inner critic, thinking, *"this is just the way that I am."* They end up believing, *"I am my own worst enemy."* If the resistance can get you to be at war with yourself, then you'll be sent into a lifetime engulfed in a conflict of *"you against you."*

DEFEATING THE INNER CRITIC

For centuries, people have been trying to kill these self-beating thoughts by debating them; attempting to argue against these parasitic thoughts. Well-meaning believers shout from rooftops with militant aggression and a warfare-like posture, in order to break free. Although aspects of this can be helpful, tactics of force alone can at times leave you discouraged and exhausted. This type of battleground needs a more refined approach.

I spent years trying to fight these self-attacking thoughts with aggressive repentance and deliverance tactics. There is nothing wrong with utilizing those methodologies. But I learned first-hand that the only way to defeat the inner critic is to infuse your heart with an immersion in the love that God has for you. Only love can drive out this self-destructive inner dialogue.

To really overcome the inner critic, you have to learn to have a better relationship with yourself. This must begin with learning how to love yourself the way that God loves you. I share about this in great detail in my book, *"God Loves Me and I Love Myself!"* To experience the power of transformation, you defeat the inner critic by flooding your heart with God's love for you.

LEARNING THE PRESENCE OF LOVE

One of the greatest ways we are invited into the beauty of God's love is found in the second pillar of love--kindness.

Love is kind.

Remember, patience is what love can handle. Kindness is what love gives out. When you meet someone who is loving, you discover the power of the love they possess through the kindness that radiates off of them. It's not just the words they say. It's the posture they carry and the aroma surrounding their words that settle your heart into relationship.

When someone constantly acts and responds in kindness, you want to be around them. Kindness sets the atmosphere of relational interaction. It is also the catalyst for long-term transformation to occur.

The key activation is that you need to learn to engage kindness towards yourself. When you look in the mirror and relate to yourself, every thought and word needs to come under the influence and domain of kindness. Immerse your inner dialogue with kindness and you have now set yourself up to experience the healing and freedom your heart desires.

LEARNING THE LANGUAGE OF KINDNESS

So how do you actually experience this?

It all starts with addressing your self-talk, the inner dialogue that follows you all day long. You live with a built-in narrator that interprets everything you experience. Whether you acknowledge it or not, you have an all-day story playing on auto repeat within your thoughts. It sets the tone for how you see God, yourself and the world around you.

Most of your self-talk is probably very negative and self-rejecting. If you live in autopilot, a swarm of disempowering and unkind thoughts will follow you from the moment you awake until you sleep.

I spent many years of my life living under the constant influence of these thoughts. At first, I began renouncing the various spiritual attacks that made me an enemy to myself. Self-rejection, self-hate, self-condemnation and self-contempt were at the top of the list.

Although this was helpful and got things started, my heart began to turn a corner when I welcomed the new inner dialogue into my life. I interrupted the negative self-talk with a new track of kindness. I made a firm decision to speak kindly over myself, which opened my heart to love like never before.

THE INVASION OF KINDNESS

To apply the power of kindness, ask yourself, *"What would it look like to engage your thoughts with 100% kindness? What would your day look like if you allowed the kindness of God to infiltrate your every struggle and challenge of life?"*

I know this will be a game changer for you. Coming into agreement with God's kindness will revolutionize your transformational journey. In fact, the Scriptures remind us to not treat the kindness of God lightly. It carries God's love and goodness towards you, leading you to change like nothing else.

Or do you think lightly of the riches of His kindness and tolerance and patience, not knowing that the kindness of God leads you to repentance?
Romans 2:4 (NASB)

Many Christians think of repentance as a groveling apology towards a God who is angry. Yet the most powerful turnaround you can experience will come out of a response to God's loving kindness towards you.

When you taste of Father God's kindness towards you, it drowns the opposing thoughts that train you to be harsh, condemning and negative towards yourself. Counterfeit temptations no longer become desirable when our hearts are filled with God's genuine goodness and kindness.

WHAT IS GOD SAYING?

To make this even more practical, I work diligently to help people tune into what God is speaking to their hearts. Hearing from God can be a really challenging and difficult subject for many, often because they've not been equipped to experience the kindness of our loving Father. Without the context of God's patience and kindness, we won't understand what it means to relate to God.

As you discover the kindness of God, you can learn how He relates to you as His child. His river of transformation flows through His kindness, goodness and love. Just when you think you have completed your discovery; a whole new sea awaits you.

God speaks through His Word, but He also brings a witness to your heart through the Holy Spirit, who is known as the Comforter. The Spirit relays the heart of God's kindness in bringing instruction and comfort to your life.

I can give you all kinds of helpful instructions about what you need to focus on for your healing and freedom journey. But if you tune into the main theme that God is working on, you will immerse yourself in the power of His flow. Then, transformation becomes less of a self-help grind and more of an exciting adventure with God.

But here lies a problem. When you ask believers, *"What is God saying to you in this season of your life?"* many are hesitant in their answer. Some will blurt out a bunch of religious rhetoric that sounds nice, but they are just covering up for the fact that their real answer is, *"I don't have a clue."* While others have a reference for God that omits His kindness. They hear everything through judgment, condemnation and shame.

In my one-on-one work with believers, many of them have a distorted lens of God. So, asking them, *"What is God speaking to your heart"* can trigger a "taskmaster god," a "nothing is ever good enough god" or a "god that you always run and hide from." It can unleash an inner voice that is not of God, which prevents them from moving forward in a healthy way.

WHAT DOES LOVE SAY?

One of the helpful ways I have learned to hear from God and detox those counterfeit voices is to ask myself, *"What does love say?"* This fine tunes my heart to learn how to hear from God, because His love permeates everything He does with His children.

To the believer who is seeking to walk in the truth of God's Word, this is a safe question to ask because God IS love (1 John 4:16). When you discover the power of what love really is, you gain an understanding of God's nature. So, it can be really helpful to ask yourself, *"What does love say?"* or to ask, *"What does kindness say?"* because kindness is the way God addresses us.

I know off the bat, some can react to this advice with apprehension, as many have a distorted lens of what love means. This is a legitimate concern. Pointing to a counterfeit love has given a false permission to live outside of God's morality and led others into deep deception. I am equally grieved about this escalating problem. Modern society is losing touch at lightning speed with the truth that sets us free.

But this cannot negate an important precept. Truth needs to operate within the context of love. The Apostle Paul's admonition to *"speak the truth in love"* (Ephesians 4:15) shows us that the power of truth needs the conduit of love for truth to have its intended impact.

Truth is like a copper wire with intense voltage. On its own, truth can become a weapon that is used to accuse and damage people unnecessarily. I am sure you have watched many Christians use truth apart from love. It becomes like a live wire, firing off intense voltage and surges of electricity in unpredictable patterns. You cannot even get near it because there are high odds you will get electrocuted.

But place that wire into a rubber conduit and you have now channeled that power into its intended flow. That's how truth operates. God does not slap you in the face with His truth. He does everything through the conduit of His loving kindness towards you. In fact, God has a way of correcting and even chastening us in a way that is empowering, because it is all done through relationship, built on kindness.

Loving kindness never dilutes truth. It gives the environment by which truth operates in its fullest potential. Jesus says He is the truth, which shows us that our knowledge of truth is not a connection to concepts, but relationship with a person. You cannot have healthy relationship without loving kindness.

Being connected to the power of the truth which sets you free needs to be founded on loving connection to the Father, Son and Holy Spirit, while granting that loving kindness to immerse your thoughts. Heart healing will never happen when the kindness of God is not priority.

GAINING FRUITFUL CLARITY

With some helpful coaching, most believers can discover that they can and do hear from God. Often times, they just need to ask in the midst of their struggle, *"What does love say here?"* or *"How can I apply kindness to what I am going through?"*

Tuning into God through his nature of loving kindness is how you build a foundation of relationship. From there, all the other aspects of intimacy are built off of that base. In the midst of kindness, you will gain the perspective of heaven over your life and even your struggles.

Have you ever swam in a beautiful part of the ocean, where, with a good set of goggles, you can see underwater for hundreds of feet? It allows you to take in the beauty and majesty of where you are, while also having clarity on where you are headed. You cannot see forever, but you can see far enough to get perspective and direction.

If suddenly, a surge of waves kick up the sand, seaweed and other oceanic debris around, suddenly you lose your visibility as the water quickly becomes murky. Swimming under these conditions can be incredibly challenging. But once the sand and debris settle to the bottom, you can compose yourself and regain clarity over your swimming experience.

The same is true with your heart healing journey. The harder you are on yourself, the murkier your vision will be. Without kindness, you cannot see your situation through God's eyes. You'll see everything worse than it really is. Inner tension will build, anger will rise and discouragement will swell.

Without kindness, you'll lose perspective. That is why a soothing word from a friend can calm a raging storm in your heart. You are responding to the nurturing power of kindness.

BEING KIND TO YOURSELF

The days of beating yourself up need to come to an end, right now…today. You've wasted enough hours, days and years beating yourself up. Why not let the kindness of God take over?

But this will not happen on its own. You need to bring your thoughts and emotions into agreement with God's kindness towards you. And one of the best ways you can engage that is through speaking kindness to yourself.

The best way you can steer your self-talk into a new direction is by speaking loving words over yourself. I recommend you develop a simple list of kind statements you say to yourself on a regular basis. Your tongue is a rudder, so use it to steer your heart into love.

This will help you to learn the language and cadence of God's love. The good news is that you can begin experiencing that right now, in the midst of your difficult battlegrounds. Don't make it worse by being hard on yourself. Take in a deep breath…pause…and start speaking to yourself words of kindness.

QUESTIONS FOR CONSIDERATION:

1. What does the inner critic sound like in your own thoughts? What does it say?

2. What would it look like to experience kindness towards yourself?

3. Make a list of five kind sentences you can begin saying over yourself on a daily basis. Practice this for 30 days and see what kind of a difference it makes in your heart healing journey.

PRAYER:

Father God, today I make the decision to bring my thoughts into alignment with Your love towards me. I thank You that Your love is rich and deep, built on the power of patience and kindness. Today I choose to receive Your love and to give that love towards myself. I open my heart to receive Your kindness and hear Your loving thoughts.

Today, I break agreement with the inner critic, those thoughts that come against me and seek to keep me from receiving Your love. Today I take a step into Your patience and kindness. I choose to express kindness over myself. I renounce the belief that I am my own worst enemy. I choose to live in the power of loving kindness. I thank You Father that You are kind towards me and I receive that with an open heart. Thank You for Your love. In Jesus name I pray, amen.

RECOMMENDED RESOURCE:

God Loves Me and I Love Myself!
(Book and Online Course at markdejesus.com)

16:
Kicking Out the Inner Pharisee

Then Jesus said to them, "Take heed and beware of the leaven of the Pharisees and the Sadducees." Matthew 16:6

Growing up, I listened to condemning thoughts all day long, which included guilt, shame and regret. I often obsessed over these thoughts and feelings, especially because I was trained to believe that my standing with God was at stake. These thoughts led me on an unfruitful journey of religious works, self-pressure and constant fear that I was not "right with God." It welcomed the voice of an Inner Pharisee that grew as the years went on.

I have to admit, it took me a long time to realize that God does not condemn His children. He does not use condemnation as a way to speak to His kids or try to develop them. But religion and the lies of the enemy have trained us to lean our ear to the condemning voice, leaving us with an Inner Pharisee that doesn't want to leave.

When you grow up perceiving God in His holiness without a grid for loving relationship and connection, then you always wind up feeling afraid, intimidated to approach Him. You're left feeling unworthy and never good enough.

On top of it all, the condemning religious Pharisee does not let you come near heart healing. It trains you to believe you don't need it, keeps you in the buzz of performance living or it makes you feel so unworthy of ever receiving the depth of God's healing love.

PREVENTING GRACE AND LOVE

It can be really hard to engage heart healing if you have a lot of religious condemnation being hurled into your thoughts all day. For many who grew up in a law-based or legalistic environment, their hearts are easily condemned. It steals their confidence and clouds their hearts with a lot of confusion.

The condemning voice of the Inner Pharisee seeks to block you from receiving all that God has for you. If love and grace are not the foundation of your relationship with God, then the voice of the Pharisee will gain front-row seats in your thoughts. Black and white thinking will easily rule the day. Perfectionism, performance and the pressure to get everything right will be driving forces. Your past will be a haunting presence that taunts and disqualifies you, rather than being experiences you can learn from.

From my years of work with Christians, I am convinced that a large majority of tender-hearted believers are under the barrage of condemning thoughts. I was one of them. Growing up, the prevailing message was to "live right" and "do what is right." Holiness was a major emphasis. Though these precepts are legitimate and needed revelations to learn, they are out of place if not laid on the foundation of love and grace. In my heart, I was missing the reality of God's unconditional love for me. To me, grace was a word that meant that God tolerated me. My foundation was off.

Without grace and love being experienced in our hearts, everything in our spiritual structure will be distorted. Certain Scriptures won't make sense. Most of all, this setup will give rise to the voice of the Inner Pharisee; a deceptive religious friend that will keep you from receiving all that God has for you.

CONFUSION AND MIXUP

Many confuse condemning promptings as God's correction or conviction. Some have even been trained to believe that the worse you feel, the more God is working on you. This stems from an unhealthy God lens. You are not listening to God, but the voice of the condemning Inner Pharisee.

During a personal heart renovation season, I knew I needed to mature in how I perceived God's voice. I realized that the majority of what I thought God was saying to me was really guilt, accusation and shame. I needed a whole makeover in my listening.

As I expressed this problem with others, one after another, believers nodded their heads, sharing that they battled with the very same thing.

CHANGING MINISTRIES

The Apostle Paul called the Old Covenant, based on the law, the "ministry of condemnation" (2 Corinthians 3:9), which has such a lesser glory than the covenant in Christ Jesus we can experience today. For much of the New Testament, the Apostles had to bring the body of Christ out of law-based thinking and living, so they could experience the ministry of righteousness, founded on the grace of our Lord Jesus Christ and the love of Father God.

I realized I was listening to the wrong ministry. I was sitting under a religious framework that was still keeping me in performance-based Christianity with perfectionistic undertones. One day I realized, *"I need to listen to a new ministry!"*

THE COUNTERFEIT CONDITIONING

Listening to condemnation leads people to feel shame over their sin issues and obsess about their mistakes. It will further drive you to narrowly focus in on and ruminate over flaws in your life with a defeated mindset.

In this counterfeit atmosphere, Scriptures accuse more than empower, because of the condemning lens that is at work in your heart. The Bible becomes a weapon to stab yourself with, instead of a sword to set you free. Give that harsh, accusatory voice your attention and it will grow louder. Self-analysis will become unproductive and you will find yourself in spirals of unfruitful repentance and confession. Your heart will be conditioned to obsess over where you are falling short, rather than rejoice over the new identity God has given you.

Listening to these thoughts will never lead you to freedom, but we seem to follow them, nonetheless. The Inner Pharisee hijacks our ability to discern and leads us into a life of little power or fruit. Believers become more rigid and heavily burdened under this yoke. Most of all, your heart will feel empty and dry, as your ability to receive from God feels blocked.

REGAINING MY CONFIDENCE

Condemnation prevented me from receiving the beauty of God's grace. In fact, I spent about two years saturating myself in what grace and love meant, while learning to detox the condemning voice of the Inner Pharisee.

Overwhelmed by what I was up against, I found myself landing in 1 John chapter 3. This passage saved my sanity.

> *For if our heart condemns us, God is greater than our heart, and knows all things. Beloved, if our heart does not condemn us, we have confidence toward God.*
> 1 John 3:20-21

As I read this passage, it became clear to me that my confidence had been stolen by condemnation. It was affecting my relationship with God and stealing my ability to walk with empowering faith. My perspective became darkened by my flaws, while losing sight of the power found in God's grace and the price Jesus paid for on my behalf.

The revelation in this Scripture passage propelled me to get my confidence back. I began to filter out the accusing thoughts of condemnation. I made a decision to permanently break up with the abusive Inner Pharisee that was putting me down and shaming me all day long. This act of faith cleared up my heart to hear the voice of God and His leadings built on faith, hope and love. The airwaves over my thoughts became clearer than ever.

ONE-TWO PUNCH

Condemnation is part of the one-two punch the enemy brings your way. He ushers in a thought and gets you to think or act on that thought. Then he condemns you for participating with the thought. Most come under that guilt and shame, vowing to never do it again. After a short time, you repeat the same sin.

That is because condemnation never leads you to freedom. Only grace and love, with truth can set you free.

When you come under condemnation, you get into the boxing ring with the accuser. Whenever this happens, you will always come out with a black eye. That is because the enemy never plays fair. He uses evidence of your past, getting you to believe a narrative that is not lined up with how God sees you. You will lose your energy and get bogged down with black and white thinking that leaves no room for grace, process and relationship. You are always left feeling defeated.

THE POWER OF BREAKING OFF CONDEMNING SHAME

In John 8, I am amazed at how Jesus dealt with the woman caught in the act of adultery. The Scribes and Pharisees, which represent the ministry of condemnation, used this moment to execute punishment to the full degree. One of the greatest signs that you are in the presence of religious condemnation is when you feel unsafe and uncovered.

In one response, Jesus was able to remove the spirit of condemnation, more specifically, shame, from the atmosphere, by replying, *"He who is without sin, cast the first stone.* (John 8:7)"

This remarkable statement leveled the playing field and exposed the hypocrisy they all lived with.

But allow me to look at this a little deeper. With one step, Jesus also set this woman free from her sin. He asked her to look around and see if anyone was accusing her. As she looks around and replies, "No one," Jesus leaves her with one sentence, "Go and sin no more."

Wait . . . what about dealing with her issues? This was probably not her first sinful sexual experience. Don't we need to deal with her father wounds? I am sure she was neglected and abandoned by her dad. Some counseling would help. Don't you need to do some inner heart healing work so she can stop this pattern? Maybe a year of some good Christian therapy to help her heal and recover?

That wasn't given here. Just one sentence of grace was all she needed.

Jesus knew that her greatest problem was a condemning shame. It was shame that actually kept her in a place of fear and hiding. She probably vowed to stop this behavior, only to be led back into it again. It was the voice of love and grace, in the light of God, that ushered in the freedom that she needed.

So, if one sentence that broke off condemnation and shame would set the heart of an adulteress free, imagine what it could for any other battle you and I face in our lives?

I CAN SEE CLEARLY NOW

When under the barrage of condemnation, you cannot see yourself or your battles clearly. You don't know what you are up against and you will remain in a continual loop of bondage until love and grace enter.

Under condemnation, you cannot even get to the root system that reveals why you even go down destructive pathways in the first place. You will be so preoccupied with the panic of feeling shamed, unclean and guilty. The enemy knows if you experience love and grace, your heart will be unlocked to step into true freedom. You'll see your battleground with greater clarity and even uproot the broken issues of the heart that keep driving you into wrong directions.

Condemnation focuses on getting you to follow the rules better. Love and grace invite you into relationship, so that you are changed while experiencing who God is. Condemnation keeps you focused on your flaws, while grace empowers who you are in Christ, expanding each place of your heart that heals and matures in who you really are.

YOU ARE QUALIFIED

When I look over the history books, God didn't use people because of how sinless or perfect they were. In fact, I see God doing great things in spite of how flawed they were.

This never means that following God gives us a license to sin. Quite the opposite. When you taste of the goodness of God, any counterfeit option cannot even reach the foothills compared to the vast mountain of God's unending love.

But in order for healing of the heart to have its work, we have to let go of self-righteousness and religious performance, to realize this is all based on what Christ has done for us.

In the meantime, God works powerfully in you, even though you are weak, flawed and struggling.

Your qualification comes in what Christ has done and what the Father says over your life. Tuning into this means shedding the voice of condemnation off of your back. You don't have to listen to it, because the enemy is not the one who qualifies you to begin with. God does.

Condemnation is a waste of time, especially considering that God works with you, right where you are. He even works with you in your kinks and quirks along the journey, in relationship, to grow you in His love. The only way we are changed is in the love of God.

In fact, the less condemnation has a voice in your life, the better off you will deal with those areas that need healing. You'll tune into what God is working on and leave all the other distractions aside.

QUESTIONS FOR CONSIDERATION:

1. In what ways do condemning thoughts, including guilt and shame, hinder your confidence and keep you from an empowered healing journey?
2. In what ways have you confused condemnation as being the voice of God?
3. Is there a specific thought, based on condemnation, that you need to renounce and break free from today? If so, what is it and what's the new step of freedom you need to take?

PRAYER:

Father God, I thank You that You are a good Father, who does not condemn His children. I come into agreement with the truth that You do not accuse us, nor leave us in guilt and shame. You are a Father filled with grace, love and truth; who empowers us to break out of bondage and walk freely in the power of Your light.

I realize that in certain areas of my life, I am listening to condemning thoughts that are keeping me from the freedom that is available. So today I take a stand against these lies and I choose to walk in the power of Your freeing grace. God give me the strength to cast down the Inner Pharisee and jump into Your loving arms.

I declare today that condemnation is no longer welcome in my life. I open my heart to the power of God's love and grace. Thank You Jesus for making a way for grace to be a real work in my life. I choose to step into that and walk free from the chains of religious performance, perfectionism and constantly being put down. Today, I make a new agreement with the love and grace of my Father in heaven. In Jesus name I pray amen.

17: Permission to Feel

And He took with Him Peter and the two sons of Zebedee, and He began to be sorrowful and deeply distressed. Then He said to them, "My soul is exceedingly sorrowful, even to death…" Matthew 26:37-38

Heart healing is useless if you do not allow yourself to process feelings in a healthy way. When you experience life from the heart… you feel. Healing gives us permission to feel and process the emotions we are facing with safety and nurture.

But for many of you, it was *not* ok to feel.

For centuries, feelings have been misunderstood. On top of it all, feelings have gotten a bad rap in Christianity. Most believers I know have been trained to look at emotions and feelings with a number of unhealthy perspectives.

- *Don't pay attention to how you feel.*
- *Ignore your feelings.*
- *Don't speak out negative feelings. It means you validate them or make them permanent.*

Although these statements have some well-intentioned motives behind them, it left us abandoned in how to process the emotions of the heart. We need to go deeper, so that God can heal us and mature how we deal with our emotions.

Understand that there is truth to not allowing certain feelings to dictate your life. There is also wisdom in not letting every ebb and flow of emotions drive us into following them. That can certainly become dangerous.

Deceptive patterns can develop, where:

- *Every wave of emotion has significant meaning that must be followed.*
- *Because you feel something, it means that specific emotion is "who you are."*
- *Every emotion rules your mindset and decisions.*
- *Because you have an emotion, it must mean God is trying to tell you something.*

Although falling under the changing waves of emotions is unhealthy, it is equally dangerous to the life of the heart to ignore emotions that are signaling pain, heartache and troublesome issues you need to face.

GOD HAS FEELINGS

A brief reading through the Bible will give you endless examples of people whose emotions were expressed in a variety of ways. Celebrations, joyous festivals, weeping, sorrow, grief, sadness, pain and more were all part of the journey that many biblical characters we admire expressed.

In the narrative of Scripture, especially in the Old Testament, you see the emotional expression of God in a variety of ways. Many people are found saying, *"Wow, God seems really upset."* But then I look into their eyes and ask, *"Have you ever been upset about something that wasn't right? Does sin bother you? Does it upset you when you see other people suffering unjustly? Then why do we find it odd when we see the emotional expression of God towards these heart-breaking manifestations?*

Is God a robot, where nothing touches or moves Him? Of course not. But aren't you made in the image of God? If you have feelings and expressions of emotions, doesn't God have feelings?

Let's get to the real issue. Do we not allow ourselves to learn from the emotional expressions of God simply because we do not allow ourselves to experience the spectrum of emotions in our own lives?

HEALING TWO EXTREMES

To get a better perspective on emotions, we need to heal two extremes we can fall into.

1. Becoming victim to every wave of emotion.

If we are honest, most of us wake up and just go with what we're feeling. We live more as thermometers, that read the temperature, rather than thermostats that set the temperature.

Those who live as victims to their emotions become limited by what they feel in the moment, leading them to lose perspective on their journey. They have not been taught how to nurture challenging emotions, so their spirals lead them into further ditches. Emotions become a driving force, often stealing emotional stability; at times robbing a person from connecting to grounded perspectives.

Those with sensitive hearts can easily fall into this pattern. You can become so tied to an emotion you are struggling with, that without proper training, you can easily fall into emotional nose dives that are unproductive for your health.

This was the ditch I lived in for so long. I carried such a sensitive heart, yet had no idea how to walk through the spectrum of emotions that I faced with a heart that is equipped. I lived with a lot of shame and defeatism over how I felt.

Without proper nurturing, one can feel that the challenging emotions they face are a permanent part of their journey, even coming to a conclusion of, *"this is just the way I am."* It can leave you believing that the troubling thoughts and emotions you face are a permanent fixture in your life.

2. Ignore, suppress and deny your feelings.

Those in the other extreme appear to be stronger and healthier, yet their only difference is the ability to hide or suppress what they are feeling. Their unaddressed emotions go down underneath the surface.

Denial is a big part of this lifestyle. Deniers often look down on Christians that are expressive. The term "emotional" becomes a negative label on people who feel. They are seen as unstable and to be avoided. In response to people they see as "too emotional," the deniers find a ditch of deception on the other side. Their hearts are numbed out, leaving them disconnected.

Sadly, you can be deceived into thinking you can get by in life by disconnecting. But those emotions go somewhere. Avoiding them will lead you to a world of problems down the road.

It's actually impossible to think without feeling. Every thought you have carries a corresponding emotion along with it. Both of these two extremes do not allow you to process emotions in a healthy way. Whichever ditch you find yourself leaning into, this often comes out of what was cultivated in your formative years.

GETTING A BETTER LENS ON EMOTIONS

There is a better way to look at emotions, by seeing them with an empowered lens.

1. Emotions are a part of life.

The truth is, you cannot have a thought without an emotion. This is what makes us human beings. We think, feel and experience. Certainly, there are many thoughts that can lead you astray, but approaching thoughts with a black and white hostility can lead you to missing the beauty that is found in emotions we avoid, like grieving, sadness, disappointment and sorrow.

2. Engaging emotions is done best in the atmosphere of self-compassion and grace.

Most feel shameful about what they are going through or feeling. The emotions they face create a lot of shame and self-contempt. In this heated emotional furnace, we lose sight of what God may be up to underneath these emotions.

The only way you can develop true self-awareness and get to the root of why you feel the way you do, is to connect to the power of self-compassion. Learning to love yourself as God loves you allows you to see what's going on with greater clarity and wisdom.

3. Give yourself permission to feel the spectrum of emotions.

In the atmosphere of self-compassion, this is where you can live more alive from the heart like never before. Jump starting your heart healing journey happens best when you give yourself permission to feel, not just "positive" or "upbeat" emotions, but the negative ones you seem to run from all the time.

It is time to become more "ok" with emotions in general. Whichever ditch you find yourself leaning into, recognize that you can feel your emotions in a healthy way without moving into dysfunction.

For many of you reading this, there are unwanted emotions connected to pain that you never allowed yourself to feel. Spiritual and emotional maturity is not about pushing away unwanted or negative emotions. It's more about discovering God in the midst of what you are feeling. He doesn't depart from you when you are having a bad day. In fact, He is just as near in those painful, uncomfortable and even awkward places.

Have you ever been sad and just allowed yourself to be sad? What about anger? Have you let yourself feel the anger and allow God to meet you in that? Have you avoided grief, only to see that area of your heart act out in unwanted ways?

It's time to give yourself permission and invite God to meet you in your emotions. Feelings do not have to dictate your decisions, but they can help you to become aware of what might be going on in your life.

4. Just because you feel something in the moment, doesn't mean it's permanent.

Psalm 30:5 reminds us that weeping or sorrow lasts for a night, meaning that it doesn't need to stay forever. But we do need to process through it. Sometimes people are so afraid of certain thoughts, thinking that will permit them to stay forever. The lie that can often slip through is that if you are feeling a certain emotion, it means that it will always be there as a permanent component to your life.

5. Find safe people to process with.

In the context of tribal connections with friends and family, God designed this to become the home base where you can process what you are going through.

It's amazing how a safe conversation with someone can put your emotions in their proper perspective. You find yourself and regain your composure, simply by sharing with someone who listens, understands and empathizes.

6. Discover with God what's underneath those emotions.

If you spend your time avoiding certain emotions, you may miss out on healing what's underneath. There are often underlying reasons why you are angry, sad or depressed. But if you spend all your time trying to get rid of these emotions, you may never discover an issue that God can heal.

So next time, allow the emotion to come to the surface, but invite God into this place. Allow Him to show you with His truth what's going on in your heart that needs healing.

7. Lead your heart.

There is much dispute amongst Christians about the heart. Do we have a new and pure heart? Or is our heart deceitful? Which is it and what can I trust?

In my study of the Scriptures and experience in life, I have found that there are valid points to both perspectives. I don't want to assume that everything that pops up in my heart is 100% pure. I think it's naive to believe that. Yet at the same time, I cannot ignore the desires that spring up from the heart altogether. The journey of awakening your heart involves connecting to healthy desire.

I think the best posture that can move you towards a healthy direction is to lead your heart. Set the compass of your heart with God's truth. Allow the Holy Spirit to search your heart and let your real motives come to the surface. David prayed this.

Search me, O God, and know my heart… Psalm 139:23

QUESTIONS FOR CONSIDERATION:

1. Do you find that you are an emotional thermostat or thermometer?
2. Do you feel that your emotions always drive you in your decision-making?
3. Do you feel there are areas where you avoid your emotions?
4. Of the seven steps mentioned in this chapter which one do you need to apply today?

PRAYER:

Father God, I recognize that You are a God who feels. You created me in Your image and I want to learn what it means to live out of a healthy emotional heart. I ask You to give me wisdom in knowing how to navigate through my emotions. Reveal to me where I fall victim to emotions that dictate my life and decisions in negative ways. Show me where I end up suppressing and denying emotions that I need to face.

In it all, I ask that You help me learn how to live with an open heart that experiences You and life to the fullest. I know that through it all, You will be there with me, so I put my trust in You. I know You will help me to live from a healthy and free heart. In Jesus name I pray, amen.

18:
Receiving the Signals from Emotional Pain

The spirit of a man will sustain him in sickness, but who can bear a broken spirit? Proverbs 18:14

Physical pain can lead us to realize that something in our body needs attention. But what about emotional pain? Are we equipped to address the signals of emotional pain that rise up?

When someone has a physical injury, we immediately know what to do. We engage medical treatments, emergency rooms and physical therapies to restore strength and movement. But have we been ignoring the emotional pain we carry?

Most people do not even know they are in emotional pain. It often takes someone who has to point it out. But even when it's brought to the surface, most are left saying, *"What am I supposed to do with this? Life goes on, so, whatever...."*

Therefore, we continue to walk around with a growing tank of pressurized pain that is unaddressed and therefore, unhealed. The pressure slowly builds over time, but there is little awareness as to what that pain may be pointing to.

Even if one realizes they have issues of emotional pain, most of the time, the best answer folks have is to "soldier on" and ignore it, saying, *"What else is there to do?"*

But there is so much more available if we can learn to face our emotional pain with God.

WHAT IS EMOTIONAL PAIN?

So, what is pain? To keep it simple, *emotional pain involves experiences in our history that have affected us negatively and are having a present influence in our lives.* These areas of woundedness stem from past relationships and can prevent us from living in healthy patterns. Pain can also be a present pressure, burden or hardship that is taking a toll on you. For many, emotional pain can keep a person stuck, unable to move forward.

In order to move in a more fruitful direction, we need to learn some things about pain that will actually help your heart healing journey and keep you from feeling stuck.

1. PAIN MANIFESTS ITSELF IN MANY WAYS.

Pain does not always show up in tears. Most of our pain manifests in ways we don't realize. The following symptoms can often be related to unaddressed emotional pain:

- Relational disconnection
- Anxiety
- Depression
- Numbness
- Isolation
- Addictions
- Restlessness
- Irritability and anger
- Mood swings
- Sleep issues

- Excessive drivenness & intense striving for achievement
- Obsessive and/or compulsive thinking patterns and behaviors
- Perfectionism
- Chronic busyness

2. IT CAN BE EASY TO IGNORE THAT YOU ARE IN PAIN.

In my personal work with people, they are often surprised to realize that the battlegrounds they face are a sign they live in unhealed pain. That is why it is so important to receive helpful feedback. Those who love us and are heart aware can provide input that unhealed pain is crying out, but hasn't been addressed.

3. PAIN IS A SIGNAL THAT THE HEART NEEDS TO BE ADDRESSED.

Like warning lights on the dashboard, pain is a signal that issues "under the hood" need to be addressed. Most people keep the gas pedal to the floor and never pull over for the daily, weekly and monthly pit stops we need to process the pain of life. We only seem to address it when we've gone past the warning lights.

A really powerful way to start healing more effectively is to see pain as a helpful signal, rather than something to ignore or suppress. We see pain as such a nasty thing, we spend our lives eluding pain and running towards comfort as much as possible. Others sulk in their pain unproductively, with little remedy, growth or progress. Instead, view pain as a place to address issues that need healing and maturity.

4. PAIN HAS A SOURCE.

If you run from pain, you may never learn about what's at the source. Follow the pain and it will lead you to a theme of hurt or emptiness that has been following you. The healing of pain often takes discernment, so that you can discover the root issue that needs to be addressed in your life. Usually pain directs us to a place where love has been compromised in our lives.

5. FACING PAIN WILL STRETCH AND STRENGTHEN YOU.

If we face the pain, the result can be a strengthened heart with greater resilience and fruitfulness. Most people are capped off at the level of pain they are avoiding.

I wish it were true that we grow best in comfortable times. But the reality is, our greatest transformation can be discovered through seasons of adversity.

The truth is, you actually need adversarial situations to bring out the gold that is in you, provided you lean into the learning that is available. I find that in every trial, there is an invitation for a certain area of our heart to be developed. Growth and character need to be enhanced, provided we don't run away.

In my early years of facing pain, God spoke to me. *"I want to take you into the spiritual gym of what it means to heal and strengthen your heart."* I realized that my spiritual and emotional muscles were weak. Facing pain in more effective ways was going to bring out the man of God I was created to be.

6. REMOVING YOUR DYSFUNCTIONAL PAIN MANAGEMENT.

The best way you can face the pain of your heart is become aware of the habits you go to in order to numb yourself or escape the pain of life. Remove the way you typically cope and you will be able to discover the pain that you've been avoiding.

Stop your drug of choice. Stop viewing pornography. End the chronic busyness. Stop the comfort eating. Don't go for that glass of alcohol. Pull back on your constant church busyness. See what's there. It may be really uncomfortable at first, but you may discover some powerful opportunities for your heart to be healed like never before.

7. INVITE GOD INTO THE PAIN.

As the pain rises to the surface, instead of running to an addiction or coping mechanism, turn to God and invite Him into your pain. Many times, your pain can involve broken perspectives you have about God. Maybe the very issue of inviting God into your pain brings up a wound that says, *"God is not here. He doesn't care about me. He is distant."* Whatever the pain may be, it is time you face it and work through new mindsets and habits that will help you heal.

ADDRESSING THE SHUT DOWN

For many of you, a key to bringing your heart back to life involves dealing with your "shut down" responses. Life gets tremendously hard, showing no signs of getting any easier. In the midst of this turbulence, there seems to be no other option.

You are tempted to shut down when you feel you have reached your threshold of experiencing pain. The problem is that we learned the shutdown mechanism so early in life, we never had the ability to flex our heart muscles to grieve and heal from the pain we have faced.

The "shut-down" is conditioning people to live more like zombies than humans that are alive. The deception is thinking you can actually function with a shutdown heart. It can seem that no one notices, but over time, the hardness will creep through.

When you are shut down in your heart, it may not always be outwardly visible right away. You can go to work, pick up your kids, make dinner, attend church and go to the gym, all with a heart that is shut down. You can even participate in ministry. But deep down inside, there is a numbness and coldness that is enveloping.

Over time, there becomes a disconnect to have true heart engagement with God and others. Your relationships lose depth. Your connection to God seems distant. Your marriage moves into roommate syndrome and you feel disconnected from your kids.

Cynicism and bitter roots grow and there becomes a hardness to life and hope.

TURNING THE BREAKER BACK ON

When we shut down, we are first deceived into thinking that we can only shut down the breaker in our heart that deals with pain. We then scratch our heads as to why we cannot connect to the emotions that we really want--joy, peace, love and hope.

This is because in the heart there is only one breaker. You shut down because of one area, but it triggers a chain reaction that shuts down the whole system. Millions hit the "shut down breaker" and attempt to carry on without dealing with anything.

That is why the door to feeling again and awakening your heart to life can begin with one decision that says, *"Today, I make a decision to turn the breaker of my heart back on. I choose to face the pain I was avoiding, so that I can become the person I am destined to be."*

QUESTIONS FOR CONSIDERATION:

1. What area or areas of your life have become a place of pain in your heart?
2. What are some unhealthy ways that you respond to pain?
3. In what way do you find yourself shutting down your heart?
4. Of the seven points mentioned in this chapter, which one will help you the most right now?
5. What is a new way that you can face your pain in a more empowering way?

PRAYER:

Father, I thank You for Your love that provides safety for me to face and heal from my pain. I recognize that there are areas of pain that I need to stop avoiding. I cannot suppress them any longer. I realize that it can be so easy to use a pursuit of knowledge as protection from becoming vulnerable and addressing the pain of my heart. It can also be easy to get lost in my head and lose what it means to be connected to You from my heart.

So, I make a decision today to face the pain that is in my life and allow You to meet me in that pain. I ask that You help me to see the issues of my heart that need healing and maturing as I confront the painful areas of my life. I pray that I would experience a greater depth of Your Love and discover connection with You in a way I never did before. Meet me in my pain, heal my heart and set me free into an empowered life. In Jesus name I pray, amen.

19:
Stuck in Your Head

Knowledge puffs up... 1 Corinthians 8:1

In the early stages of my son Maximus' life, we received a gut-wrenching diagnosis that he was on the autism spectrum. This sudden and unexpected turn of events sent us into a nosedive of grief and sorrow, but also a passionate cry for strategy in how to battle for him. As I began to tenaciously pray and fight for him, I found myself immediately praying for his brain.

Seems to be the obvious choice, right? Yet as I looked to God for direction and instruction, I sensed a statement coming back to me that would be important for Max and the masses of people that I have been able to influence.

"Don't just focus on his brain. Pray for his heart." This statement was profound, because it revealed how we so easily focus on symptoms and neglect directing our attention to the core place of a person's life; the heart.

"STUCK IN YOUR HEAD"

One of the modern plagues I am observing is the masses of people that are "stuck in their heads." They are either lost in the details and overwhelm of life, or they use an accumulation of "head knowledge" as a way to cover up their brokenness. Many have settled for an intellectual and analytical approach to life that in many ways has disconnected them from the life of the heart.

Let me make it clear that I am not promoting a lifestyle that dismisses rational thinking, while floating into a mindless abyss. I am also not advocating that you turn off your mind. I am more about realigning the flow of where you relate and connect from. I want to implore you to get out of your head and love powerfully from your heart.

When you get stuck in your head, a number of negative symptoms can manifest:

- You will focus on accumulating knowledge, without actually experiencing it.
- You will seek for a quick fix and instant results.
- You will focus on symptoms and never get to the root problem.
- Your knowledge can cultivate an arrogance that keeps you from humbling yourself.
- You never actually connect with God. Your focus is on learning knowledge and information, without actually experiencing who God is.
- Your relationships lack connection, because living stuck in your head keeps you from becoming vulnerable and authentic in your relationship interactions.
- Your knowledge and intelligence can become a cover for the fact that your heart is shut down.

USING INTELLECT AS PROTECTION

One of the classic ways people avoid vulnerable, heart connected living is by becoming highly intellectual. We pursue knowledge and present a sophisticated and erudite persona that can impress people. Yet deep down, we are broken and hiding.

It's easy to rely on knowledge alone for your sense of safety. You don't have to deal with brokenness or vulnerability. Just focus on information and data. It can help you grow big businesses, organizations and even churches. Yet deep down inside, there is a heart disconnect.

The number one cry for Christians that come to me is they know about God's love in their minds, but they recognize they are disconnected from it in their hearts. This reveals our need to slow down and become more relationally wired. We are filled with information in our heads, while still empty in our hearts.

Empty hearts that choose intellectualism can win arguments, possess impressive resumes and showcase staggering presentations. Yet they still feel unfulfilled. Their degrees and accomplishments are wonderful, but there is an emptiness in the heart that has not been touched.

Deep down, they are slowly becoming bitter, angry and cynical, yet they cover it over with cognitive processing and impressive articulation that veils their bitter roots. If you are able to peel back these layers, they will express they understand the things of God in their head but lack it in the heart.

GET BACK TO THE HEART

If we're going to have the life that Jesus said we could, a life that overflows from the heart, we have to allow the Father to heal our hearts. But we have to remember, Jesus came to heal the broken hearted, not the broken headed.

In the Old Testament Scriptures, there was no word for mind. It was all about the heart. The emphasis on the mind came about in the Greek culture, where intellect and knowledge were elevated to high levels of status. The simplicity of child-like faith became clouded over.

The Old Testament word for *heart* taught people to learn by experiencing truth and engaging it with your full self. This caused truth to be imprinted on the hearts of people. Faith was not a class you took; it was an experience with God. Mentors and friends processed with you, where you learned how to walk with God as you walked with each other. This gave room for you to marinate on truth and live it out.

MAKING THE CHANGE

So how do we make the shift? Here are some suggestions.

1. Get more honest and vulnerable.

The only way to freedom is to get honest about where your heart is at and vulnerably share it with others. This will take humility, where you first admit to those around you that you struggle to connect with your heart. The path of change opens up when you just get honest about what you are wrestling with.

2. Let your lack of heart connection motivate you.

What will you do with the fact that your heart is disconnected and you are lost in your head? Will it lead you to further cover it up, or pursue a new path of learning that allows you to engage God with an awakened heart?

3. Stir up a hunger.

The only way you will change is when you are hungry for change. But most who are stuck in their mind and disconnected from their heart often say, *"I want the passion, but I just don't have it."*

If you find yourself in that position, ask God. Honestly tell Him where you are at. Call out to Him and ask for a hunger and passion that you struggle to have right now. Believe that He will meet you where you are and yield to the grace that He sends your way.

4. Seek to *experience* truth.

Don't just settle for learning information. Knowledge is meant to be applied, experienced and encountered. Sometimes it starts with simply admitting, *"I know about certain subjects, but I need to experience it with my heart."*

For example, most people know *about* the love of God, but have little experience of His love in their life. Therefore, they stand as a spectator in the things of God, not as an active participant.

So, to live more heart connected, seek to experience what you learn. Instead of just taking a class on prayer, engage in a 30-day prayer experience. Go on a spiritual retreat. Start a journaling habit. Sign up for some spiritual and emotional coaching.

5. Slow down and learn to connect.

The pace of living heart connected is a much slower pace. At times, it can really frustrate the fast pace of our data-driven, information overloaded society. When you slow down, you can actually make space to deal with what your heart needs to address.

6. Focus on what brings the heart back to life.

For some people that I have coached who are heart disconnected, I have at times encouraged them to reformat some of their dead-end habits. So, don't be afraid to reboot your routines. Don't follow religious rituals that leave you empty. Find ways to engage God's Word and prayer where you are connecting from your heart. Prayer may need to be spent more in silent receiving, stillness and reflection. Bible reading needs to be built around seeking to experience what the Word of God points to.

7. Be open to input.

You cannot make this change by yourself. To live more heart aware and awake, you will need the input of mentors, counselors or coaches who can equip you. Be open to what they have to say.

Humble your heart to become teachable, so that you can move into a whole new way of living.

QUESTIONS FOR CONSIDERATION:

1. Where do you find yourself learning information without giving yourself space and time to experience it?
2. Using the seven steps given in this chapter, how can you get back to the simplicity of heart connection in your life?

PRAYER:

Father God, I pause right now to slow down, so that I can be more connected to relationship with You from my heart. I recognize that the pace of life can lead me to accumulate information without the experience of transformation. I want to be more connected to the heart You gave me. I want to truly experience life from the heart.

I ask that You help me today as I learn to live more from the heart and not just from information in my brain. I realize that information alone will not lead me into full transformation. I need to experience truth.

Jesus, You are the truth, so I position my heart to experience You more. As I learn to get still, pray and digest Your Word, I ask that You help me to experience the truth that will set me free. Father, I thank You that You love me so much and I look forward to experiencing more of that love with my whole heart. In Jesus name I pray, amen.

20:
Learning to Grieve

Blessed are those who mourn, for they shall be comforted. Matthew 5:4

Many consider grieving as something we only do when we lose a loved one. This is certainly an important aspect of grieving. But grief is not just about the loss of a loved one who passed away. There are a number of experiences in life that we need to grieve as well.

True grief is an experience given to us by God to process loss of any kind. If done in a healthy way, grieving can be a powerful exchange with God to lead you through seasons of pain, mourning and sadness.

You cannot live a life on earth and ignore grieving, or it will catch up to you. Over the years, I have found that there are many times in our life, where we need to grieve the loss of:

- Certain expectations or plans that didn't work out.
- Dreams that did not come to fruition.
- Relationships that were precious to us and are now gone.

Grieving can also include processing the painful experiences you've had. You may also need to grieve the loss of something you needed in life but did not receive. Regardless of what it might be specifically, a powerful healing experience is learning to grieve through what the heart is aching about.

SIGNS YOU HAVE NOT GRIEVED

I have watched many walk through the pains of life without pausing to allow their hearts to grieve. Deep wounds do not just go away. You can ignore them, suppress them or keep yourself so busy you never have to think about them, but someday the unhealed pain will rise.

Many see grieving as a sign of weakness, so they sidestep the process, projecting themselves as emotionally "strong," only to find the ungrieved issues springing up later in life. Many people consider pausing to grieve as a waste of time. Some even think that allowing yourself to grieve will make you more selfish, self-centered and dangerously introspective.

Sadly, the real driving force is that we are uncomfortable with grief. Too many in Christianity hope that over time things will get better and go away. Time alone does not heal. Intentional healing and allowing yourself to grieve makes way for the heart to heal.

Here are some common battlegrounds that can manifest when someone has not grieved:

- Anger and irritability.
- Intense blaming in relationships.
- Striving and hyper-driven behavior.
- Addictions
- Apathy, numbness and checking out.
- Mood issues or depression.
- Fatigue or burnout.

WHAT MAKES GRIEVING SO HARD?

Besides the fact that it is painful and uncomfortable, there are a few reasons that make grieving challenging.

1. We are not prepared.

Experiencing loss of any kind is something you are never perfectly prepared for; mainly because it is sudden and unfamiliar.

2. We don't have models.

Do you know of anyone who has grieved well? If you do, then count your blessings, because most people don't have good examples for grieving.

3. You don't allow yourself to grieve.

If you are hard on yourself, then grieving will bring out that self-contempt with intensity, never allowing you to have the permission and space to grieve.

4. You think it's weak or bad to grieve.

You might be afraid that you will dip into becoming a victim or you may see grieving as a sign of weakness.

5. It is inconvenient.

Let's be honest, grieving creates a great deal of disruption in our lives. We don't feel we have time for it.

HOW TO GRIEVE IN A HEALTHY WAY

But there are beautiful treasures of healing and growth found in the trenches of healthy grief. Many people ask me, *"How do I grieve in a way that is productive and helpful in the long run?"* In the years of facing my own heart issues and helping others process through grief, here are some things to consider.

1. Make the decision to pause and feel what you need to be feeling.

Slow down and take a pause before life makes you slow down. It often first begins with simply acknowledging the pain of a loss. Maybe you've lost a meaningful friendship and never paused to grieve it. This happened to me many times. I was so used to living in performance mode, when friends left, betrayed or moved on, I compartmentalized it and moved on without a thought.

Over time, it caused me to become more disconnected to the pain I was feeling, because I was determined to never let what people did to me, get to me. This led me to a series of denial fueled responses that eventually caused me to crash.

2. Practice loving acceptance of what you are feeling.

This stage cannot be skipped over. Otherwise, you'll beat yourself up and consider the whole grieving process to be stupid and useless. The reality is, you may not be used to giving yourself room to process pain. But you need to.

So how do you do this? Start by feeling what you are feeling without instant judgment and assessment. Let yourself feel the painful thoughts in the presence of God's love. Give yourself compassion to feel what you need to feel. You may need to talk it out with a good friend or a trained person who knows how to walk through this.

3. Find your best way of processing the pain.

Grieving is often done well through tears, but it doesn't have to be the only way. Journaling your thoughts, talking it out with someone or taking time to get in solitude and breathe can be great ways to engage what you need to face. Jesus said there is a blessing for those who mourn (Matthew 5:4) so it's important that you see the mourning involved in grieving as a good thing.

4. Give yourself time.

The Psalmist cries out that our *"weeping may endure for a night, but joy comes in the morning"* (Psalm 30:5).

It is important to note that the "night" may not be an 8-hour window. Every issue the heart needs to grieve does not get solved by morning. In fact, for some, you are actually going through a "night season."

The time frame on this is different for everyone, but if you give yourself the gift of patience, saying, *"It will take as long as it takes,"* you allow the kindness and patience of God to flood your heart. It also begins to welcome a joy to flow into our lives that cannot be stolen.

5. Watch over your hope.

Biblical hope is more than just "I hope this works out." It is your divine perspective that impacts everything in life. In the midst of grief, the enemy seeks to infiltrate, discouraging your process and ultimately stealing your hope. When your hope has been stolen, your ability to see your future with God looks bleak, negative and hopeless.

Paul reminds us in 1 Thessalonians 4:13 that we as believers can grieve without losing hope. You may have seasons where everything seems to go black, but you can know that your hope doesn't have to be lost. It may be going through renovation; to the point where you may think all hope is lost. But know in the midst of this trial, God is in the business of reforming and strengthening your divine perspective.

6. Lean into the learning.

In the midst of grieving, there is often a jewel of learning and growth for your life. Healthy grieving has a way of adjusting us to a much healthier lifestyle. New mindsets and perspectives are needed. These changes would never happen if we didn't experience the treasures found through healthy grieving and mourning.

7. Give God your pain.

When we grieve in a healthy way, we engage a powerful process of exchange with God. We hand over to Him the sorrow and pain of our life, while opening our hearts to receive the beauty that He has for us in the midst of these difficult seasons.

For so many, there is tremendous maturity and power that flows through those who have learned to take their deepest pain and emotionally give it over to our loving Father. In the presence of a divine exchange with God, He will remain with us and deposit amazing treasures that no one can steal.

> *To console those who mourn in Zion,*
> *To give them beauty for ashes,*
> *The oil of joy for mourning,*
> *The garment of praise for the spirit of heaviness;*
> *That they may be called trees of righteousness,*
> *The planting of the Lord, that He may be glorified.*
> Isaiah 61:3

QUESTIONS FOR CONSIDERATION:

1. Is there a loss in your life that you have not taken the time to grieve in a healthy way?
2. What makes grieving challenging for you?
3. What aspect of grieving do you need to give yourself permission to experience?

PRAYER:

Father God, I thank You for being so gracious and kind to me. I thank You that You never leave me nor forsake me. Your grace and kindness empower me to grieve through any kind of loss in my life. Even though the pain of loss can be intense, I know that You are with me and will walk with me through it all.

I ask that You give me the courage to grieve through the losses of my life that I need to face. Help me to slow my heart down so that I can make a powerful exchange with You, as I give You my pain and You deposit in my heart the strength that I need. I pray that through the grieving process, I will discover a deeper journey in my life I never knew before. Walk with me through this all I pray, in Jesus name, amen.

21:
Healing Memories

And they overcame him by the blood of the Lamb and by the word of their testimony… Revelation 12:11

Do you remember your first day at school?

What about your first romantic experience?

Do you remember your wedding day?

What was your first day on the job like?

What is the happiest moment of your life?

What was your most painful experience?

These questions will all bring up specific memories in your life. The thoughts connected to those memories will also activate a series of corresponding emotions. It's how you relate to or associate with those events in your history. The emotion connected to the memory is what will influence you to return to it for comfort and gratitude or avoid it because of its discomforting effect.

The interpretation of your memories will become a motivating influence on your entire journey. In fact, many of your perspectives and even decisions were propelled out of how you processed certain life events.

YOUR STORY

Your memories influence the story you carry around in your heart. It's the narrative that you listen to every day, which influences your perspective and the decisions you make. Everyone carries a story in their hearts that is either empowering or disempowering their journey.

The Bible uses the word "testimony" to describe the inner story that you and I are called to carry. A testimony is basically the "story" of what God has done in your past, what He is currently doing in your present and what you know He is doing regarding your future. How you process your testimony will greatly impact your trajectory.

Your testimony is also your greatest asset for impacting this world for good. The sharing of what God has done and is doing in your life cultivates an invitation for others to experience the same great fruit in their own life.

The power of your testimony begins with God's healing work on broken subjects connected to the past. For all of us, there are memories that need God's love, grace and truth, so that the associations we've connected to those memories can be matured.

At times, memories that need healing arise as flashbacks. In other cases, they can appear in relationship interactions, where someone brings up a past event, triggering an awareness that your heart needs to address an issue. There are also those times where we feel a deep agitation, irritability, anger or anxiety that is connected to a memory that God needs to heal.

Many times, the memory that needs healing will come to you, providing you are open. When you are teachable and humble, you can receive the signals for healing that will change your life forever.

This is great news for the open hearted. But unfortunately, the topic of addressing the past brings up a lot of arguments amongst Christians.

THE PAST IS THE PAST

When you engage heart healing, one must learn to be ok to process past events. Yet one of the biggest arguments brought up against dealing with issues of the past is the phrase, *"the past is the past, so leave it in the past."* The problem is there is often a driving force of avoidance involved.

Many people are scared to bring up the past. They have shoved life events and experiences into a box and tied a pretty bow around them, so no one can open it up. Past the layers of glitter and shiny wrapping paper, there are areas of unhealed pain that have chains of condemnation, guilt, shame and fear tied to it.

IT'S UNDER THE BLOOD

In my pastoring days, the subject of addressing issues of the past would trigger discomfort in certain church members. They would come up to me after a particular service and say, *"Mark, I don't need to talk about the past. It's all under the blood!"* Although this declaration sounds biblical at first, this statement can be a classic Christian method of escapism, to avoid talking about uncomfortable issues that are connected with the past. It actually reveals that deeper healing is needed.

But why do we run? Isn't God the safest person in the universe to talk to about anything? The "it's under the blood" comment revealed a well-rehearsed protection, but it's missing the point. God is not out to condemn you, shame you or expose you. He is a loving Father, who loves you so much that He wants to heal you.

But He will lovingly bring certain subjects into the light, so He can walk with you through them. When people would defensively say, "It's under the blood," I would often respond with, *"That's wonderful! Then that means you should be able to talk about these things anytime. When we let God's cleansing blood wash us, His blood is a healing blood too.*

So therefore, you should be free to talk about what God did in that area of your life."

The problem is, they were still hiding in shame. It's not under the blood if its hidden under the carpet.

True freedom arrives when we are able to talk about the past in the safety of love and grace, while allowing God to heal the root issues that are connected to those experiences.

If someone is truly free, they can talk about it. It is one of the signs that healing is taking place. But it takes allowing God and safe people into those areas, so the healing can occur fruitfully.

But if we walk in the light as He is in the light, we have fellowship with one another, and the blood of Jesus Christ His Son cleanses us from all sin.
1 John 1:7

WORKING IT OUT WITH OTHER BELIEVERS

The most powerful place to work out our personal history should be in the context of church family. At the same time, church interactions can also be the very place where some of our deepest hurts can be experienced.

The New Testament church was set to be a key location, where we can each process out our lives in safety, grace and love. James even instructed us to *"Confess your trespasses to one another, and pray for one another, that you may be healed…"* (James 5:16)

Quite often, the healing you need is involved in confession; not by laying out a list of sins, but in allowing someone to hear about and connect to your journey. If they are safe and mature, they will actively listen, stand with you and encourage your journey towards healing.

But we cannot experience this if we keep running from our past.

OUT OF CONDEMNATION AND INTO GRACE

Another common roadblock that many carry is a condemned perspective about their past. A defense mechanism kicks up that says, *"I am forgiven. I don't need to talk about that."*

For them, the idea of addressing an issue of the past means that God has not forgiven them. Furthermore, talking about the past brings up a great deal of defensiveness, because deep down, there are thick layers of self-condemnation and shame.

Many families cannot experience the healing they need, mostly because they don't know how to have non-condemning conversations with each other. This leads them to not even bother talking about issues. As one person said to me, *"Our families never fight. We just get divorced ten years later."*

It is always counterproductive when an event of the past is brought up, only to be met with a knee jerk response of, *"you are condemning me"* or *"you are telling me I am a bad person,"* even if you are communicating with the utmost kindness and humility.

If condemnation is ever in the mix, healing in relationships can almost never occur. Just blame, anger and chronic arguments will arise.

God never condemns us in our brokenness. But He is also a loving Father that wants to address those issues with His kindness. But be aware, condemnation will seek to filter your past experiences, so that you are never free to talk about an issue or walk through the healing your heart needs.

When you are wired into the life of grace, it gives you the ability to talk about anything. Grace allows you to face any issue and address any subject, knowing you are never condemned or put to shame. You know in your heart that you are safe with God.

In grace, you realize that life is all about cultivating empowered relationships, with God, yourself and others. And one of our greatest needs in building grace relationships is talking out aspects of our story that need healing.

A FREED PERSPECTIVE

I have worked with so many people who were deeply troubled by their past. Healing was so challenging, because their lens was dominated with the voice of condemnation. It took a restoration of God's love and grace, bringing the person to a new foundation of relationship, for freedom to open up.

You don't have to be ashamed in this process, for God uses every aspect of your journey, even your wounded past, for His glory. For most people, this statement doesn't ring true in their day to day thoughts. We think God uses our feats of strength and only tolerates our weaknesses, sins and struggles. Learning to live in His love and grace makes all the difference, for in that atmosphere, God revolutionizes our hearts.

THE GREATEST MEMORY HEALER

If you have unpleasant and challenging memories of the past, one of the first steps towards your freedom is to engage the power of forgiveness. In learning to heal, awaken and strengthen your heart, none of this book will mean anything if you do not learn to forgive.

I have observed that without forgiveness, wounded hearts are often pushed into further torment and can be left stuck. Unforgiveness welcomes bitterness, which will keep your heart toxic and defiled. The pain of what happened can remain with you continually. That is why at various stages of our life, each of us need to learn the power of forgiveness.

But don't mistake it. Forgiving is not always easy. At times, it will challenge you to the core, testing you with the deepest pains of your life. But it is also one of the greatest ways to unlock your healing journey.

Forgiving someone may not instantly remove all the pain of everything that happened. There may still be areas that need grieving. But forgiveness jump starts the healing process in dramatic ways. I have found that although forgiveness is a decision, it often needs to be processed out in stages. I have also found it to be true that when someone refuses to forgive another person, they end up piling up toxicity within themselves.

I encourage every person to walk through layers of forgiving their parents, because most of our wounds trail back to how our relationship was formed with them. When we choose to not forgive them, we give permission for the sins they battle to repeat in our own lives.

If you struggle to forgive, you may need to connect to what it means to be forgiven by God. It can be so much easier to forgive others when you truly understand what you have been forgiven of. You give out to others what you have processed in your own life.

You may also need to forgive yourself. When you actively forgive yourself, you say "yes" to God's forgiveness and you welcome the power of God's grace to kick out the shame, condemnation and guilt that wants to replay over your heart.

Making progress over painful memories does not mean that those memories never affect you. The greatest victory over your past circumstances and experiences is to gain God's perspective over them. When His thoughts become your thoughts, your story gains God's interpretation of your life that empowers faith, hope and love in a way that impacts others with great power.

QUESTIONS FOR CONSIDERATION:

1. What is the main theme that plays over the story of your life? Does it empower you or disempower you?
2. Are there certain subjects regarding your history that you find yourself avoiding?
3. In what ways do condemnation, shame and guilt keep you from empowered healing?
4. Where is forgiveness the most challenging? Receiving forgiveness from God? Forgiving yourself?
5. What kind of difference would it make if the grace and love of God infiltrated every aspect of your story?

PRAYER:

Father, I thank You so much for Your love and grace towards me. I acknowledge that You are using my past and present towards a powerful future, as I allow You to work with it all. So, I give You permission and access to work on all the areas of my heart and life, knowing that You are kind and patient with me.

Thank You so much for providing a safe place in Your light to receive the healing that I need. Help me to shake off the shame that keeps me from being able to experience Your deeper healing power. Give me the courage to step out into relationships, open up and receive the greater healing my heart needs. In Jesus name I pray, amen.

22:
Healing from Trauma

God is our refuge and strength, a very present help in trouble. Psalms 46:1

Delving into the work of transformational ministry, I've encountered the growing number of people who've had significant traumatic events in their history. This left them with a tremendous amount of internal battles and unhealed emotional pain. The collateral damage from trauma is having a widespread impact in our world.

Of the highly influential subjects that pertain to heart healing, none of them has brought the issue to the forefront more than trauma. There is a growing awareness of how traumatic events impact our minds, bodies and our overall emotional health. But there is certainly much more work to be done.

If you look around an average congregation, workplace or community, a large percentage of people have been impacted by traumatic events, but you would never know it. Many traumas are incredibly intense, such as experiencing abuse, being exposed to war or serving as a first responder to horrific situations.

At the same time, there is a large percentage of people who have experienced trauma, but don't realize it. They can be innocently unaware as to the influence of these negative experiences. They often shrug off these life events as irrelevant to their current battles.

Getting yelled at, shamed or being suddenly removed from a group can be traumatic. In addition, many have lived under a traumatic life, where their upbringing was filled with constant stress and tension, like the example of living with a parent who is an addict. Whatever the situation may be, we all have to become aware of how traumatic events may have an influence on our spiritual and emotional health.

WHAT IS A TRAUMA?

A trauma is a sudden moment of intensity that takes you off guard. It shocks your system. In a traumatic moment, everything happens so quickly, you are not able to sort through your thoughts or respond in ways you'd like to. Your mind and body initiate an instant reaction in response to the event. Many times, your reflexes engage without your conscious, active thought.

A trauma will trigger a person's "fight or flight" mechanism, which can lead some to gain a laser sharp focus, in order to deal with the threat at hand. Their body gets ready to "fight." Others go into "flight" mode. Their stress response engages an anxious, fear-based reaction, where the main goal is to get away and find safety. Many find themselves emotionally frozen under the weight of the moment.

We are all affected at different levels of intensity by trauma, depending on your wiring, coping mechanisms and patterns of life before the traumatic event even occurs. Your body is designed to handle certain traumatic moments with protective responses and reactions that help you to gear up and deal with the sudden moment. It's the "aftereffects" that are troublesome.

Your mind and body were not designed to hold the impact of those events inside of you. There is no permanent place within you to store the effects of trauma. The pain, pressure and destructive thinking that can form as a result need to be detoxed out of your system.

The deadliest impact of trauma can be when destructive thinking can settle in and take deep root within our hearts. Our ability to process love, peace and relational stability can be hampered tremendously by a traumatic moment.

My goal in this writing is to encourage you to open your heart towards healing the negative impact that trauma may have had on your life. It is not to give you a replacement for any professional help you are receiving. I want to support you with some practical and helpful tools that can empower your healing journey.

COMPASSION WORK TRAUMA

Much of my understanding of trauma has come out of working in the trenches and helping people process through excruciatingly painful moments in their life history. At times, hearing the nightmares of people's traumatic experiences took a toll on my own emotions. I had to learn how to process what I heard in a way where I could keep myself grounded, while at the same time, working through some of the most horrific experiences people have had.

I also learned very quickly that when you roll up your sleeves to help people, there are times when they will strike back. Some of these became sudden and traumatic, as I discovered first-hand how much unhealed brokenness was hindering the life of the church.

There were those who twisted things I said and verbally attacked me, those who wanted to lump me up with their past abusers and those occasional times I felt physically unsafe around some of the people I was asked to help.

I have also experienced the traumatic pain of encounters with unhealthy ministries and churches; some of them being very cult like behind the scenes, who lashed out in abusive ways that shocked me. These traumas awakened my eyes to the unhealthy church world that can exist behind closed doors. Some of those harsh experiences took quite a bit of time to recover from. Others, I am still working through the healing process.

ALLOWING THE HEALING PROCESS

One of the common cries I hear from those who've experienced trauma, is they often dream for some kind of special technique, or secret remedy to quickly alleviate the pain, confusion and torment that trauma can leave behind.

Many seek for the perfect spiritual encounter, hoping the right prayer from the right person can give them the quick relief they need. Others chase after the right method or approach, scouring through scores of practitioners who promise that their technique is the most effective. So many are driven by the thought that if they can just find the silver bullet solution, it will make everything better.

We are often led to this because we haven't given ourselves permission to heal in a journey or process. Recovery takes time, but we want it to happen quicker, so it becomes easy to think that we are missing something. I never want to discourage a passionate pursuit of healing, but I must emphasize that you cannot avoid the *process* and *time* it takes to recover. The key is not so much what approach you take on trauma, but that you exercise patience and compassion on yourself as you heal.

When trauma hits your life, it impacts you on three dimensions. You become spiritually, psychologically and physiologically impacted. Those three levels of who you are, need to be addressed. Your spirituality needs connection with God to open up His healing power over your heart. Your mind needs renewal and resolve under the power of God's love and truth. Your body, which is usually the last part to land into healing, needs reconditioning into what it means to live in safety.

My greatest encouragement to the healing of trauma in your life is to first allow yourself patient time to heal. I also exhort you to engage how God designed you to recover from traumatic events.

1. Get perspective.

In my work helping those who have been impacted by trauma, my primary goal is to provide a safe environment, where they can effectively process what occurred and move towards gaining a healthy perspective. Without a proper perspective on your traumas, you'll either shove them down into a deep pit or soak in the toxicity of pain without any progress.

Healthy perspective is everything. It welcomes the kindness you need, so that you can heal under the umbrella of compassion. A healthy perspective welcomes the patience of God, so that you don't come under pressure to hurry the healing process. A grounded perspective will keep you on a steady path of healing.

A loving mentor, coach or counselor can help to provide a healthy perspective, so that love can have its deeper work to help you recover. If you are blessed to have a friend, small group or a tribe of compassionate people who understand you, these can be safe places to process your pain and gain a healthy perspective for your journey.

2. Learn to make exchanges with God.

No matter what has happened to you, there is a Father in heaven who wants to take your pain and exchange it for healed fruit. In my darkest moments of painful experiences, I learned the art of making an exchange with God. When I didn't know where to turn or make sense of what I experienced, I started by verbally giving over what I felt to the Father. Without filters, I poured out my emotions to Him, while allowing myself to receive His healing.

Isaiah 61 is all about making an exchange with God, where we give Him our pain and injuries, while receiving His healing balm and nurture. The exchange is powerful:

- *Consolation for those who mourn.*
- *Beauty given in the place of ashes.*
- *The oil of joy given in exchange for your mourning.*
- *Praise that will replace heaviness.*

3. Practice stillness.

One of the most fruitful tools you can access right now is the practice of stillness, the power of quieting yourself. In a world where traumas abound, the negative impact of these events are worsened by our fast-paced, busy and chaotic world. The constant movement and "go-go-go" living does not help our heart and body recover. With this in mind, you will need to make a decision to insert stillness into your daily life.

Those who have recovered best from trauma have often learned the power of stillness, where they can settle their hearts into the promise of *"Be still and know that I am God"* (Psalm 46:10).

Stillness is a loving act that allows your whole being to engage healing and recovery. It is an opportunity to settle into God's restorative power, where He can, as Psalm 23 says, *"lead you by the still waters."* It is there where He can *"restore your soul."* Some things can only be accomplished in the environment of stillness.

In stillness, you slowly restore the power of safety back into your life. You have the opportunity to communicate, *"I am safe"* to yourself, where you give that truth time to settle into your body. As you take in deep breaths, you allow your heart to come into agreement with the peace and rest of God that overrides every traumatic storm.

4. Learn to talk things out.

The worst thing you can do for any trauma you've been through is to suppress them and not talk about them. By far, one of the best and most proven helps for the recovery of trauma is the ability to talk it out in a safe setting.

I believe that most of the battle with trauma is shame. It drives us to hide and look at our traumatic experience with contempt. When we talk with someone and feel safe as we share, it takes off the power of shame and we can begin processing what happened. Each time we talk through it, we learn something new about our healing process and where God wants to restore us.

Until you talk things out, many aspects of the experience can remain trapped up in your body. Talking it out in a healthy way will allow you to gain the healthy perspective you need amongst safe people.

5. Renounce destructive agreements.

As you talk out your pain in a safe setting, be aware of the destructive agreements that have developed; mindsets that at first seek to create protection, but can be detrimental to your long-term emotional health.

I had one particular meeting that shocked my system and was traumatic for me, where I was verbally attacked by someone. The experience emotionally shredded me. As I walked away from this painful encounter, I was left with a perspective that said, *"I was not ready for that. I need to be better prepared next time. I need to protect myself."* Although this can sound logical at first, there was a fear-based influence and self-preservation behind it that was not healthy. It put me in survival mode, erected walls over my heart and kept me hypervigilant for a while. I kept looking around the corner for when the next person would attack me in that same manner. As I let myself heal with kindness, I slowly let go of that agreement, so I could allow myself to experience the joy of relational connection.

You may actually need to break agreement with, or repent of, certain strongholds that have been in place since the trauma. Fear, guilt, self-hatred and rejection are a handful of tormentors that need to be removed with God's perfecting love and truth. Activating forgiveness while plucking out bitter roots will also propel your heart into greater resolution and clarity.

6. Restoring desire.

Trauma can have the ability to damage our hope, where our perspective can become weak and tainted. It's like you wake up most of the time with a cloud of darkness that seems to veil over so much of your perspective. This damage of hope can have an impact, right down to your physiology.

Hope deferred makes the heart sick, but when the desire comes, it is a tree of life.
Proverbs 13:12

I remember working with one particular woman over the phone who had a life filled with traumas of every kind. Abuse ran wild in her history. As I documented her life, I filled an entire 4x6 foot white board with significant and damaging experiences. Her exhaustion was evident, and my heart broke over the loveless experiences she had.

As I scanned the board of traumas, I had a quiet conversation with God under my breath. I knew that trying to address each incident was going to be exhausting and overwhelming for both of us, so I listened for the most fruitful question God would have for the healing process.

After providing a safe place for sharing and processing over a number of sessions, we arrived at an important question.

"What is it that you want?" I asked.

Her reply was very revealing. She said, *"You are the first person in my life to ever ask me that question."*

Her traumatic experiences conditioned her to come under the desire and vision of everyone else, while neglecting her own power to choose. I knew that if she could resurrect her power to decide, it would give room for desire to grow and become a tree of life. Restoring desire is a powerful experience. It awakens your heart to life, empowering you to move forward, one decision at a time.

7. Engage habits that reinforce recovery.

We all have unique ways to connect to peace and healing. I want to encourage you to lovingly apply the habits that ground you back to peace. They become the "home base" exercises that remind you of God's love and plug you into restful recovery.

For me, a walk through nature connects me to gratitude and God's peace like nothing else. Some find that exercise or a hobby connects them to restoration. One of my golden habits is doing yard work. In it, I find the opportunity to physically engage my body and allow my mind to get refreshed.

As a recommendation, I also encourage you to frame your daily routine of going to bed and waking up as key opportunities to engage God and healing routines. I have found that how you start your day and go to bed are two key moments that can greatly influence your healing and recovery journey.

QUESTIONS FOR CONSIDERATION:

1. Are there any hurtful experiences of the past, which were traumatic, that you need to process through some healing?

2. In what ways has the healing process been challenging because you put pressure on yourself to heal quickly?

3. Of the seven tips for healing from trauma, which one can you begin applying today?

PRAYER:

Father God, I thank You for Your love and power to heal and restore my heart from the impact of traumatic moments in my history. There is nothing I have gone through that You cannot help me with. I thank You that You are a safe and loving Father. I come into agreement with Your safety and allow You to walk with me in the healing journey.

Today, I let go of the shame that keeps me feeling unclean, unwanted and condemned in my pain. I choose to receive Your love and grace. I let go of any thoughts and emotions that are influenced by lies, so that I can experience healing truth in a greater way. Father God, You love me. I choose to receive that love and love myself with the love You have given me.

Let Your love and peace wash over every area of my heart. I open my heart for You to do a healing work over the damaged places of my heart. I let go of fear, stress, anxiety and worry that have entered because of these hurtful experiences. I let go of rejection, knowing that I am safely loved by You as my Father and I am Your child. I come into agreement with the safety of that truth and I let it settle into the cells of my body.

Father God I ask that You restore me to peace, one day at a time. I let go of the hindering mindsets that keep me stuck and do not allow me to walk forward in greater wholeness. I choose to forgive those who've wronged me. I receive Your forgiveness and cleansing over my life.

I let my body enter into Your rest so that my nervous system and organs can come into alignment with recovery. I give myself space and time to process this out and learn what it means to rest in that truth. I declare over my spirit, soul and body that I am safe with God. He is my refuge. He is my protection, my fortress. He is the One who will fully restore me.

I come into agreement Father, with Your ability to restore me. Let Your healing flow work in my heart each day as I learn to heal, recover and encourage others to experience heart healing in their own life. I say this all in Jesus name, amen.

23:
Receiving God's Guidance

He who has ears to hear, let him hear! Matthew 11:15

In the early years of working with people in one on one settings, I had a number of tools in my spiritual tool belt that I would utilize. There were specific evaluations, prayers and approaches I would walk many through in order to help them. Even though there was great effectiveness in using those resources, I discovered that God was calling me deeper; to learn how to engage Him in greater relational depth, as I learned to heal and help others experience healing.

As I have emphasized in these chapters, healing is a process. Nothing can shortcut the transformation journey. But at the same time, we don't need to make certain chapters of the journey longer than they need to be. Healing of the heart does not need to be confusing either. I believe that our brokenness makes life very complicated, but true healing involves leaning into simplicity.

God's ways of healing involve a relational connection with you, where you learn in peace and simplicity what it means to live with a healed and awakened heart. And the greatest way you can engage this is to lean into the simple themes the Holy Spirit is bringing up for your healing journey.

FIRST-HAND LEARNING

During an intense season of working with many hungry hearts, I found myself overwhelmed with the heart healing needs that were arising. So many were crying out for help. At the same time, I was diligently allowing God to work on my own healing issues. Shaking off codependency, people pleasing and false responsibility were critical while walking through the swampland of people's pain.

As I experienced more healing and freedom in my own life, I found myself landing into a more simplified approach with those I was coaching and mentoring. Rather than living under the pressure of trying to "fix" people, I simply focused on loving them, while listening for God's narrative over their life and journey. This posture yielded my heart to what God was already doing, rather than being buckled under the added pressure of delivering some magical solution.

My prayer to the Father was, *"You love this person so much, more than I ever could. Show me what You are working on in their heart. Allow me to partner with You in it."*

This mindset is one of the greatest differences that separates secular self-help from Holy Spirit led transformation. You and I as children of God have the privilege of tuning into the divine pattern that God is weaving in your life at this very moment. You may just need some assistance to help you see it.

HEARING FROM GOD

So, with one powerful question, I began to see people navigate their healing process with greater effectiveness. I would simply ask, *"To the best of your ability, what would you say is the theme that God is working on in your life?"*

Many people would reply, *"I don't know"* or *"I have no idea."* Others would say, *"I don't really hear from God that way."*

As a coach, one of my jobs is to kindly push people further, challenging and stretching their muscles to discover what they may not be seeing or hearing. At times I've said, *"If you had to give an answer, give me your best guess as to what God is saying over your situation right now."*

With slight pause and even hesitation, many believers would sheepishly share simple statements that seemed trivial or too simple to be from God. Yet they carried profound nuggets of truth and wisdom. They would almost pass them by if we didn't take the time to pay attention:

I need to learn how to receive God's love.

I need to be kind to myself.

I need to focus on what it means to be loved.

I need to slow down.

I need to learn to enjoy and be present.

I don't need to carry everyone's burdens.

This would not take long. After just a few moments of heart to heart questions and conversation, most of the time, believers can genuinely express the main vein of God's work over their life. Usually in one sentence, they can sum up the theme that God is pointing to. My goal in coaching people is to represent God's love to them and help them tune into God's narrative over their life.

WE JUST NEED EQUIPPING

Most people didn't realize they had such powerful answers at their disposal. They just needed someone to equip them and show them what they could not see. The traumas of their life left many feeling that God had left them, so rebuilding an awareness of His abiding presence is enhanced when we become aware of what He may be saying.

Some would share what they felt God was saying as "their best guess," as though it was their own assessment or opinion, apart from God. They are often shocked, not realizing the Holy Spirit was actually right in it. Others needed refocusing, as broken experiences left them in chronic confusion. They felt emotionally "all over the place" and unsettled in their journey. Christians in this predicament often get distracted by the many teachings out there or from comparing their journey to other people's process. They are often left thinking:

- *"That person got breakthrough because they fasted. Maybe that's what I need to do."*

- *"This one gave in the offering and they said they got healed after. Maybe I don't give enough."*

- *"These 21 spiritual disciplines are what I am missing."*

Most of the time, these well-meaning teachings and approaches are distractions, if they don't point someone to the personal focus God has them on. Everyone is at a different place in their healing journey. The key may simply be to remain focused on God's prescription for you in this season.

Some believers lack confidence, because they don't think they are "spiritual enough." They also believe that hearing from God should be some deep mystical experience that manifests in a supernatural delivery. This can lead them to miss out on the simple, everyday signals from heaven. They were often hearing from God but were unsure. They were conditioned to believe that the solution was a deep, complex algorithm that could only be discovered after years of intense introspection. But really the theme of heaven was right in front of them in plain sight.

There are others who believe they hear from God clearly every waking second, but are not aware of how their personal brokenness is infecting their "hearing." I've watched many believers tout their spirituality and depth of hearing from God, while they ignored the simple truths from Scripture or the obvious themes of their life that were being ignored. Their lack of mentoring and council led them into constant personal deception.

SURPRISED BY GOD'S AGENDA

The theme that God is working on over your life may not fulfill the initial expectations you have. For example, when I first began to cry out to God about the healing of my anxiety issues, I found that God was teaching me about worship. At first, this seemed unrelated to my problem, but it actually led me into a deeper level of intimacy and communion with God, whereby I was able to gain revelation at a much higher rate.

During other seasons, the word "rest" was continually flowing over my heart. Yet that seemed from natural eyes, the complete opposite for what my circumstances called for. The pressures of life were so demanding that I fell into striving, busyness and intense activity. Meanwhile, my Father was calling me to learn how to live in divine rest when everything around me seemed to be restless.

During an intense season of pastoring and longing for breakthrough, God used a trying time to teach me how to love myself the way that He loved me. My response to painful experiences was to turn inward, where a deep hostility formed against myself. I had to learn how to become kind, patient and compassionate towards myself when I needed love the most, in the midst of pain.

I called out to God to change my circumstances. He responded by leading me into a loving exchange that would impact everything in my life. I did not expect it, but when I leaned into God's narrative over my life, the fruit of it flowed.

RIGHT ON TARGET

So, here's the powerful truth: if you stay with the theme God is working on, you will ride His wave over your life, versus trying to create your own. Wherever God is working, His grace is available to empower you through it. That's why I always tell people to "lean into the grace," meaning, direct your focus on what God is up to in your life.

The spiritual resistance you face is often directed towards derailing you from the focused agenda of heaven over your life. Discouraging thoughts that "you are not making progress" or comparative viewpoints to other people's journeys all come your way to undermine the sovereign chapter God has you in.

Oftentimes, the theme of God over your current season can be summed up in one sentence.

Discover the power of God's grace.

Learn who you are in Christ.

Be loved.

Take time to grieve.

Learn who God is as your Father.

Be patient with yourself.

Learn to rest in the Father's love for you.

Quite often, the theme over your current season can even be summed up in one word. *Forgiveness. Grace. Rest. Peace. Love. Joy. Enjoyment. Release. Surrender.*

MAKING YOUR DISCOVERY

You cannot go wrong while walking on the path God is laying out for you. To discover it in a personal way, the Word of God is the best place to start. As you read the Scriptures, pay attention to what jumps out at you. Don't waste time trying to dissect or meander through subjects that are distractions. Tune into those statements that reach your heart and speak to what you are going through.

In addition, find the person you relate to in the Bible the most, the one whose story connects to what you are going through. Lean into what they learned and glean from the mindsets they cultivated. This is where you can build momentum for your own healing journey.

I know for sure that God's narrative over your life is always empowering. He never delivers a condemning or dead-end message. Everything He does is always redemptive. He can take any pain, heartache and trial and turn it into the finest masterpiece. It's just who He is.

Don't waste your time on victim storylines that keep you stuck or bitter trails that keep you locked down. God operates through faith, hope and love, so tune your spiritual ears to those frequencies. This process of discovery works safely when you can digest it with someone who is mature and can give you honest, safe and loving feedback. It really helps if they know some of your story and can take in a big picture of where you are, while providing encouragement and edification.

EXPOSING AGREEMENTS

As God's heart for you arises to the surface, it will also expose the resistant thoughts that seek to keep you from experiencing life and healing. It is at this stage that you need to be aware of those toxic agreements that hold you back.

One of the biggest calamities of brokenness is the dangerous agreements that can develop. They form in subtle, yet dangerous ways, to steal, kill and destroy the life of your heart. They are satan's way of keeping us locked down in our brokenness so that we do not experience our full potential in Christ.

The agreements that disempower our journey can be found in certain sentences that play in our self-talk over and again.

I will never break through.

God is far away. He is not involved in my life.

What I do doesn't matter.

I don't deserve healing.

Many times, there are clusters of statements, where you can see a theme at work that you can label.

Fear of Failure

Self-Hate

Unworthiness

Rejection

As you break the disempowering agreements, make room for the healed way to shine through. Let God's direction now form the agreements of your heart.

QUESTIONS FOR CONSIDERATION:

1. What are some of the disempowering agreements you have that can get in the way of your ability to hear from God fruitfully?
2. Take some time to pray over the season you are currently living in. What seems to be the narrative of God over your life? What is the theme that keeps popping up that you need to pay attention to?

PRAYER

Father God, I thank You that You are a God who leads and guides, as I live out this journey with You. I open my heart so I can learn to hear Your voice and trust in the work that You are doing in my life. I pray that You help me to settle into Your love for me. It is my heart's cry that each day I learn to build a growing confidence that You are leading me and directing me into fruitful places.

Today, I make a decision to let go of lies that say, "I do not hear from God" or "I am not spiritual enough to hear from You." I come into agreement with the truth that You do speak to Your children. I am Your child. I am loved by You. I have ears to hear, so I open my heart to listen.

As I live the heart healing journey, I ask that You help me to learn how to tune into Your leadings. As I read Your Word, I ask for the Holy Spirit to highlight truth that will establish my heart and grow my spiritual root system into greater depth. I tune my heart to pay attention to what You are saying over my life because I know You see me, You love me and You are directly involved in my life. I thank You so much for that and I am excited about where this journey is headed. In Jesus name I pray all these things, amen.

24:
Decisions...Decisions

Choose this day... Joshua 24:15

Everything changes when your heart experiences the healing work of God's love. Your thinking gets realigned, your perspective gets empowered and most of all, your decisions begin to change.

The love of God will empower you to make decisions from an entirely new perspective. You become less encumbered and hesitant in your journey. Fear is no longer the dominant voice. When you know you are loved, there is a self-worth and value that fuels transformation. The power of love ignites a belief system that will fuel you to make decisions that are filled with hope and steps of faith.

When I discovered the power of the Father's love to heal me and fill me, it changed how I saw everything. I realized what I had been missing for so long in my performance-driven, perfectionistic-burdened life. I ended up making decisions that would terrify others around me. But my heart was so deeply impacted by the love of God, it propelled me into a whole new way of doing life. When you breathe in that kind of freedom, even if it's just for a moment, your whole view on life changes. Once I tasted of how much I was loved, all my decisions came under the jurisdiction of that one life-changing revelation.

ONE DECISION AWAY

I have made this statement a number of times. It has proven to be true over and again. *"You are often one powerful decision away from everything changing."* One key decision can create a massive domino effect. But you won't make that powerful decision unless you love yourself with the worth and value that God has for you.

You formulate your decisions out of how you see yourself. With an absence of love, that view can be clouded over with negativity, self-loathing and tolerating the status quo. We often accept abusive situations or lower potentials, simply because love is absent. Many live underneath a ceiling of limitation, stemming from the lack of love, value and worth they are living in.

The last characteristic of love the Apostle Paul laid out in 1 Corinthians 13 is that love *"believes all things."*

God is love, and His love has a way of empowering your belief system. It can drive out the destructive beliefs you carry, while filling you with a vision that is refreshed, sharpened and faith filled.

One of the greatest signs that love is having a powerful work in your life is when your belief system gets reconstructed and strengthened. You begin to see God, yourself and others differently. Out of this, your ability to decide and choose gets revolutionized.

Most of our decisions are sabotaged because our inner belief systems are in conflict. Deep down, we have limiting beliefs that keep pounding us back and convincing us that we are not worth stepping into a greater potential. Therefore, it's like changing gears in a car when the clutch is stuck. No matter how much you "rev" the engine, you find yourself in the same patterns. Most people try to give it more gas, only to find themselves exhausted. What you need is love to empower the engine of your heart to flow the way it was designed to.

BELIEVING IN PEOPLE

One of the gifts I enjoy exercising is the power of believing in the greater potential. It's tied to the gift of faith, but it is also wired into the love that God has for you. When you know you are loved, your belief in what is possible becomes radically elevated.

People often come to me with massive histories of pain, emptiness, woundedness and disappointment. In many cases, they have become so used to their negative history, they spend a lot of time convincing me of how bad their life is. Some have even said, *"I am probably the biggest mess you will meet."*

They are shocked when I don't see it that way. Love has made too much of a difference in my life. To this day, I have not seen a history that God cannot work with and bring powerful transformation to. It's not how broken you are, but more how willing you are to learn to receive love and make decisions out of that love.

I've had countless meetings with men who felt like total failures, as they realized they had not been spiritual leaders in their home. Many found themselves dabbling with addictions, while living in emotional numbness. Their hearts were disconnected for so long, this stole their identity and confidence to rise up and make powerful decisions. This drives men into a den of spiritual and emotional passivity. When a man's confidence is lacking, making powerful decisions can seem so far away.

To rebuild a man's confidence, we first must address the believing power of love that He was not given. He needs a revelation that *"he has what it takes to lead and overcome,"* which stems from receiving the Father's love. It often takes another man to believe in him and call out that greater potential. When He can discover who He is in the power of the Father's love, his ability to rise up, lead and decide will explode.

BELIEVE IN GOD WHO LIVES WITHIN YOU

I have had countless moments in life where I didn't believe I had what it took. My perspective was limited, discouraged and worn out. It is only the love of God that resuscitated my heart and empowered me to "get back in the game." It was the Father's love that opened my heart to believe in the power of God who lives within me.

Christians often hesitate when it comes to the message of "believing in yourself." It can manifest an internal tension, which is understandable. Many are concerned about falling into a life of belief in "self" apart from God.

But when you are a child of God, living as an overcomer, you are never without God. In addition, He has put inside of you everything that you need to overcome. He believes in who He made you to be. So, it is important to come into agreement with that faith perspective.

You need to love yourself as God loves you, knowing He is always with you. He is not independent of you. Experiencing God's love will reveal the belief He has in your future. But you and I need to connect to that reality.

EMPOWERED DECISIONS

The Bible declares that *"He who is in you is greater than he who is in the world"* (1 John 4:4). But this truth is meaningless if our decisions don't line up with that.

I've had mounds of interactions with people whose lack of love has killed their belief system. They are in a dead-end situation, such as staying in a relationship that is going nowhere, remaining in a lifeless job or simply tolerating a life that they hate, but live in it, nonetheless. Over the course of time, they begin to hate and loathe themselves. In this predicament, the victim mentality becomes a driving influence. Self-pity becomes the main coping mechanism.

My exhortation is often similar in every circumstance: *when you love yourself enough to see that you are worth being loved, then you will make the decisions you need to.* You and I will tolerate everything in life at the level to which we have received the power of God's love.

TAKING RESPONSIBILITY IN LOVE

When I first launched out into transformational ministry, people were so deeply touched and refreshed by the message of the Father's love and the healing they never knew was available. People would bask in that grace and soak in the refreshing power of love that washed over their hearts. He was meeting their broken history with great loving acceptance and kindness.

But over time, a problem began to arise. People used their broken history and challenging circumstances as an excuse to not make any new decisions. A victim mentality rose up, where they used this new message of healing as a place to park and not take responsibility for their life.

This left many continuing to approach God as a disempowered victim. In their minds, He was someone who should do the work for you and make your decisions for you. This "rescue me" approach can sound spiritual, but it is littered with a victim mindset.

It was a whole new revelation for many to understand that when you receive that great love, we are now responsible to make decisions in our life that align with that love. We are no longer prisoners, but at the same time, God will not push us out of prison. The power of decision, to choose, is solely in our hands. When love is received in our hearts, it brings a message from heaven, where God is speaking confidently, *"I believe in you. You have what it takes to overcome and prevail."*

But the decision is yours.

QUESTIONS FOR CONSIDERATION

1. What one decision can you make, fueled by the love that God has for you, that could make a massive difference in your life?

PRAYER

Father God, I recognize that life is filled with a series of decisions. From this day forward, it is my desire that my decisions be fueled and influenced by the great love that You have for me. Your love has the ability to enhance my hope and faith, to see myself and my life with a whole new lens. I open my heart to let Your love influence every decision of my life, so that I can take steps of faith based on the greater potential You see in me.

Help me to come into alignment and agreement with how You see me. Give me the courage to break free from the shackles that keep me living according to a lesser identity. As I experience Your love for me, I open my heart to receive the truth that will set me free.

May that love and truth impact every decision that I make. It is time I step out of passivity and take the step of faith that I need to. I choose to live as a loved child of God. I'm grateful that You will be with me through it all. In Jesus name I pray, amen.

25: Restoring Joy

Restore to me the joy of Your salvation… Psalm 51:12

It would be amazing if I woke up every morning with an automatic setting that sprung into joy. I want to immediately leap out of bed, swirl into song and dance, while manifesting life as one continuous celebration. Every problem is met with a smile and every trial arrested by joy. But the truth is, my days do not automatically start down that path. In fact, joy often requires a lot of intentionality, effort and learning.

Maybe it is different for you. It may be that each day, you have a default setting where you awaken "fresh faced" with unbreakable joy. If it is, God bless you. But for me and the large numbers of people I have helped, joy seems to be a lot of work.

If you find this to be a struggle, there are reasons for this:

1. Your ancestors most likely went through excruciating circumstances that stole a lot of their joy. Your life started off inheriting some of their patterns and mindsets.

2. You grew up with little references on what joy looked like and how to maintain your joy.

3. There are very few gatherings that help you express and experience joy. Work can be super serious. Family gatherings can involve everyone watching television or staring at their smart

phones. Many church services can be filled with solemn and joyless rituals. In many of your routines, your joy muscles never get stretched and developed.

4. You've been neck deep with daily inner struggles or circumstances that have a mission of stealing your joy and preventing you from apprehending it.

5. We are not taught a clear pathway as to what joy is, what it looks like and how we can experience it more.

LEARNING WHAT JOY IS

Honestly, I can get weary listening to how joy is often taught. It can be portrayed in ways that convey the teacher is walking in joy twenty-four hours a day, seven days a week without a hitch. As a listener, you are left feeling defeated, because you don't experience joy in the way it is being presented.

Other times, I am confused as to what joy even looks like. Many times, well-meaning speakers seek to be authentic about their joy struggles, but you are left with a baseline message that says, *"I have no idea how to manifest consistent joy."*

Most messages that focus on joy say this:

You were made to live in joy.

You should be manifesting joy.

Get over your problems and get into joy.

What's the matter with you? Why are you not manifesting joy?

At other times, joy is defined as being different from happiness. I get what they are trying to say, but I never understood this contrast. *Shouldn't people who manifest joy also express happiness? Why are Christians being taught to ignore happiness and pursue joy, when they are not showing either?*

The Bible points us to a lifestyle of joy that seems to be absent from our modern day living. The biblical words that paint the picture of joy include, delight, gladness, pleasure, rejoicing and even happy. Biblical joy seems to be a guiding force that protects us from the pressure, seriousness and negativity that seeks to infiltrate our hearts and minds constantly.

If you look at our busy, pressure filled lives, it doesn't make much room for joy. You have to press through the inner battles you carry as well as the cultural mores of the world to guard your joy.

MY HONEST RECOGNITION

I grew up taking myself and life too seriously, so I ended up leaning into many of the serious tones in the Scriptures. My parents were raised with this and their parents did too. The generations were conditioned with a seriousness that could suck the joy out of the room in an instant. The response to life is to work hard and press into facing the obstacles in life with great tenacity. The problem is that through it all, joy was nowhere to be found.

Furthermore, in my own journey, I can get way too serious and introspective, which leaves me stuck in my head and looking at life in a way that discounts the perspective of joy. This pattern has driven me to hyper-analyze my inner life while disconnecting me from the relational joy that is right in front of me. The self-analysis in overdrive sabotages the connection to joy.

It's funny how true joy and enjoyment is not a natural reference for many, even though joy is a fruit of the spirit, a birthright of experience for every believer. Joy is inside of you, but like anything else, it needs to be activated. You need daily, intentional experiences that enhance the joy that lives within you, giving expression to the joy of the Lord that God says is "your strength." I have discovered that joy was a muscle I possessed, but it needed to be exercised and broken out of atrophy.

YOUR HISTORY AND JOY

For most, your upbringing had "joy stealing undertones." You either had painful experiences that stole your joy, or you lived within religious disciplines that undermined what true joy should be. One major reason Christianity does not manifest the joy it was destined to, is because religious legalism has often blocked it. If joy is not active and fresh in a church environment, it is because the religious spirit is present and has resisted it. Believers are left with condemning thinking, shame and guilt-ridden pressure, instead of dynamic joy.

What is your historical reference of joy? Were joyous experiences encouraged? When there was an overflow of joy, did your parents fuel it, or immediately douse it with pepper spray, conditioning you to live outside the influence of joyous living?

I remember the other day when I was lurking into serious mode, I walked up to my wife, seeing her dancing to one of her favorite songs. I don't remember the song, because I was so locked into the serious subjects in my head. The mix of my Norwegian and Puerto Rican patterns were calling me to live under a yoke of heaviness and super serious pressure. Her joyful expression interrupted my joyless ditch, but it also invited me to step into joy. But in all honesty, there is a stubbornness that kicks up, demanding that my serious tone needs to be held. In that moment, I had a decision to make. *Do I continue to live in the patterns of joyless thinking or step into the joy my wife is experiencing in this moment?*

Before you think that my wife Melissa floats in a cloud of joyful bliss, she has her own battles with this subject. Just this past week, our children were washing the car with her and were excited to help, mainly because they wanted to spray water everywhere. In this setting, Melissa can get a little too serious about the cleaning task. Her strong, yet serious Lithuanian roots of "cleanliness is equal to godliness" can easily arise. As I held the water hose in my hand, I knew it was time to experience joy in a very practical way. With a quick turn of the nozzle, I began spraying every family member, including myself. It was a step of faith, as any man who sprays his wife from head to toe with water can either end up in the doghouse or find a divine moment of breakthrough. In this case, our whole family found a moment of connection, joy and celebration that silenced the stress that came upon us that week.

I always found it fascinating when my parents would say, *"You have had enough fun for today,"* as though there was a joy and fun meter they carried with them, which measured whether or not you hit your joy quota for the day. So many of us feel that a lifestyle of joy means we are going too far out there, we are not dealing with reality or that joy is just always out of reach.

I get it. But I have found that joy can be experienced. We just may need some re-teaching and new experiences to restore the innocence of pure joy in our life.

RESTORING A CHILDLIKE HEART

Many begin life with a childlike excitement of joyous expression, only to witness it slowly erode over the years. Many of us found ourselves losing joy by the time we were teenagers and never looked back.

So, as you learn to restore joy in your life, maybe it would be helpful to reflect on when joy was stolen. For me, it was in my younger years when "being responsible" came upon me with intensity. Anxiety rose as I came under the yoke of pressure. The pressure of getting good grades and making sure I was performing well in sports was always following me. I don't remember ever sharing it with anyone, so I suffered under this yoke in silence. Everything I presented needed to be just right; to the point that fearful pressure became the ruling voice.

For example, my favorite sport growing up was basketball. Playing pickup basketball brought me a tremendous amount of enjoyment. I played it every moment I had a chance. Summer was filled with it, playing until the sun was down—to the point that I could not even see the ball anymore.

But when I joined my school basketball team, the pressure to engage the drills and physically challenging workouts overwhelmed me. I didn't know what to do with the anxious thoughts that came my way. The pressure to perform and the fear of failure consumed my heart. During that time, the pure enjoyment of basketball began to dissipate. My association with the sport turned into pressure and insecurity. My joy of the game was stolen.

FINDING ENJOYMENT

During a significant time of transition, where our family and ministry relocated from the Northeast to the South, there were a million things for my wife and I to think about and consider. The move opened up a slew of new stressors, pressures and details.

In the midst of it all, I sought for a word from God, to help keep my heart and mind focused on what He was doing in our life. In all the busyness, I felt a prompting about what I needed to focus my attention and resources on.

"Enjoyment."

Wait. What about warfare? What about being diligent? Is there a prayer strategy? What about recovery from all the exhaustion? Is there a certain way I need to pray?

"Enjoyment…be present and focus your heart on enjoying every moment you are living in."

Sounds so simple, even trivial. Yet the gold in this thought could have passed me by if I dismissed it. This one simple word gave me an open door into what joy involves.

To discover the power of joy, allow me to lead you into what helped me. Start with enjoyment. What do you enjoy? I have personally found that the recovery of joy can begin with cultivating those areas in our life that bring en-joy-ment.

Many reading this will say, *"I have no idea what I enjoy anymore."*

Bingo. That's where you need to start. Discover the simple things that help to revive what it means to enjoy again. To enjoy, I have to connect to *desire*, which the Bible says is a "tree of life." I also have to learn to be present in every moment.

In working with people who have been abused, restoring enjoyment is critical. As you depart abusive relationships, you will have to learn what it means to find enjoyment in activities that are not connected to that abusive person or environment. You have to start asking, *"What do I enjoy?"*

Biblical joy speaks to the experience of "delight." There is a delight within your heart, an enjoyment that is steady, consistent and powerful. Joy is a pillar of what Paul expressed when he wrote *"the Kingdom of God is righteousness, peace and joy in the Holy Spirit…"* **Romans 14:17.**

I believe the three feed into each other. Righteousness in Christ leads us to eternal peace. Peace sets the stage for joy to be truly experienced. In my work with people, I spend a lot of time affirming righteousness and peace in their hearts. But it is a Kingdom birthright that joy needs to be a natural follow up to the peace of God.

THE RESTORATION OF JOY

I think it is profound to observe that when David recognized his adulterous sin with Bathsheba, he penned the prayer to God, *"restore unto me the joy of Your salvation"* (Psalm 51:12*)*. Sin not only leads us into acts that harm ourselves and others, it eats away at our joy.

Could it be that at the root of our sin patterns is a loss of joy that drove us to seek for it in all the wrong places? Is the joy of the Lord a divine force that actually guards us from the lust of counterfeit pleasure?

DEVELOPING NEW REFERENCES

I have heard so many definitions and teachings on joy, but very few demonstrations of it. That's because we're only giving people theories and concepts they have not experienced. People need opportunities to experience joy, to let loose and fully engage a moment of celebration and delight.

Joy doesn't need to be an intense moment of ecstasy, but I find that we often need to be broken out of our comfort zones of mediocrity to see the greater joy that is possible. Your patterns need to be jarred into new ones.

When my wife and I were pastoring a church years ago, we felt it to be so important that our gatherings not be spectator events, but participatory gatherings, where we would be stretched to experience what God is teaching us.

With that in mind, we would at times move the chairs, kick up some high energy praise songs and encourage people to engage the posture of celebration.

It's amazing that quite often, the last place you will see a joyous manifestation is in the gathering of believers who are called to be possessors of joy. I've been guilty of it more than I care to admit. In fact, when there is an attempt to engage God and each other with joy, a religious anger rises up in many who see expressions of joy as heretical, unholy or sacrilegious. When in reality, it is way more heretical to know about joy in theory but never manifest it or experience it.

During one Sunday service, I played a Christian Country Gospel song that was filled with twangy banjo playing. At first, people smirked at me as though I had lost my mind. When in fact, I was just tired of joyless Christianity. I was weary of Christians walking into church gatherings as though it was a funeral.

So, in this "joy exercise," I had everyone get out of their seats and march around the room in celebration. The awkwardness inside of people was at an all-time high. For some, you could visibly see irritation forming as they would mumble, *"this is not what church should be!"*

At some point in the song, an atmosphere of celebration broke through. People began to laugh, dance and even shout. This wasn't a charismatic or Pentecostal church thing. It was an exercise of practicing what we knew to be true.

Our church service often kicked up a lot of discomfort because of this. Engaging joy takes effort and in reality, it can be quite disruptive to our monotonous routines. But we have tolerated learning things in our head without experiencing them. Therefore, our hearts are malnourished and atrophied from the lack of experience.

GETTING PRESENT IN THE MOMENT

One of the reasons we lack joy in our modern culture is that we're never present in the moment. The opportunity for joy is right here, right now, in front of you. Stop and soak in the privilege of the moment, to apprehend and enjoy the opportunity before you.

To experience that from the heart, I find nothing more powerful to jump start it than gratitude. I have never seen a manifestation of joy without gratitude being in the midst. Thanksgiving and gratitude help focus your attention on what God is doing, celebrating all that He is and all that He has done. It sets our attention to enjoy the moment of relationship in front of us, rather than being lost in some form of worry, dread or negativity.

QUESTIONS FOR CONSIDERATION:

1. Where has the beauty of enjoyment been lost in your life?
2. In what ways can you cultivate gratitude as you daily rebuild your connection to joy?
3. What would it look like for you to be more present in life, so that you can enjoy the relationships and experiences that are in front of you?
4. What practice can you and your family engage, that will help keep the atmosphere of joy alive in your home?

PRAYER

Father, I come to You in Jesus name, knowing that joy is a birthright given to me. You made me and designed me to live in joy. So today I open my heart to come into full agreement with living in the power of joy. I give You those places in my heart where I've lost joy. I submit areas of my life where joy was absent. I give You those moments where joy was stolen. It's time to take it back.

I ask that You restore joy in its fullest measure over my life. Today I step into joy, so that I may be strengthened by living and experiencing it. I stand against every attack that seeks to steal my joy. I give myself permission to exercise and dive into joy. I declare that I am joyful. The experience of enjoyment is returning to me now. I choose to embrace the joyful experiences before me.

I make a decision to engage gratitude and allow thanksgiving to lead me back to joy. I choose to cultivate a grateful heart, so that my joy cannot be stolen. I choose to be present in the moment so that I may experience the fullness of what is available right in front of me.

God, in Your presence there is a full measure of joy, so I choose to enjoy You and the people You put in my life, so that I may experience life to the fullest. Thank You for being my joy, creating me for joy and giving me the opportunity to take back the joy that is truly mine. I pray this all in Jesus name, amen.

26:
Living Powerfully with a Sensitive Heart

*And be kind to one another, tenderhearted…*Ephesians 4:32

A predominant theme in my heart healing journey has been learning to live powerfully with a tender and sensitive heart. At first, I wanted to figure out how to stop feeling so sensitive. However, over time, I have discovered that God can use a sensitive heart in a mighty way. It often just requires some nurture, learning and appreciation for how He designed sensitivity to flourish.

Many who live with sensitive hearts can view this trait negatively. Instead, we need to learn to appreciate and welcome those sensitivities, while allowing God to strengthen our root system. It has taken some time, but my life has been enriched through understanding my sensitive heart and nurturing it in healthy ways, while keeping the enemy from using it against me.

A SENSITIVE HEART IN THE EARLY YEARS

When I was a teenager, my youth pastor prayed over me and said, *"You have a sensitive heart."* To be honest, I had no idea what that meant or what to do with that statement. But it is true. Throughout my whole life, I have lived with a very sensitive heart. The way I processed life was filled with a lot of deep and often intense emotional connection.

At times, I was really ashamed of my sensitivity. It made me feel so different. I didn't see a lot of people around me expressing the same perspectives I felt. Over time, I actually thought something was deeply wrong with me. When anxiety, panic attacks, obsessive thinking and depression came along, those feelings worsened.

THE LIFE OF A SENSITIVE HEART

Many times people would say, *"You're just being too sensitive"* or *"You're being dramatic."* I did not just feel things, I felt them deeply. I didn't just experience things, I internalized them.

Sensitivity allowed me to express myself in the arts very well. Whether it was drama, public speaking, singing or theatre, I enjoyed the process by which I could express myself in creative ways. Having a sensitive heart made me a great communicator, but it also made daily management of my emotions really challenging.

I was very sensitive to matters of the heart, which made me passionate for God, but it also made me vulnerable to self-destructive thinking. For years, the enemy had a field day with my thoughts and emotions. Over time I had to realize that my heart was also broken. Woundedness and emptiness needed the Father's Love to heal places I didn't even know needed to be healed.

The broken areas of my heart took sensitivity and propelled it into hypersensitivity. Hypersensitivity is like having intense electrical current flooding through a wire, where it feels as though you have impulses flailing all over the place; without stable or solid connection and direction. You are deeply moved emotionally and can get easily overwhelmed and exhausted. Your senses are highly attuned; often more so than the average person.

SENSITIVE HEART AND DISCERNMENT

When you have a sensitive heart, you can easily discern the spiritual temperature when you walk into a room. But at the same time, your emotional sensitivities can lead you to become more apprehensive, reading things that are more your own personal fears and wounds, more than what is really going on around you.

Too many times, I was picking up on negative factors that were going on in me and transposing them on the people I met. When you have a sensitive heart, you can at times discern like no one else. But at the same time, you can also pick up on things that are not even there. This is why heart healing for the sensitive heart is not only imperative--it is a MUST.

Many times, hypersensitive hearts can overprotect themselves in the name of discernment. They can spend all their time "discerning" what is going on all around them, but it is really a way to protect themselves. In addition, they may not actually connect with people. With God's love and His maturation process, I allowed Him to teach me how to use my sensitivity in a healthy way, where I could truly experience powerful relationship connections.

Remember, the goal is not to turn your sensitivity off, but to allow God to ground it in His love and stability. But it takes a journey to learn how to process this authentically. Here are some ways I have learned to live with a sensitive heart and allow this trait to work for me and not against me:

1. I HAD TO VALUE HEART HEALING AS A PRIORITY.

Once I recognized there were empty and broken areas of my heart that needed attention, I passionately pursued a heart healing journey with God. Instead of running, hiding and living a hyper-busy life, I positioned myself to experience regular and ongoing heart transformation. This allowed me to begin learning what healthy sensitivity could look like.

2. I NEEDED TO GET GROUNDED IN LOVE.

The love of Father God has a powerful way of grounding us, firmly rooting us, so that we are not easily taken out by the waves of emotions that we face. The more I recognized that He loved me, the more it freed my heart to confidently flow from how He designed me to live.

When you are sensitive, it can be easy to mistake guilt, people pleasing, codependency and other dysfunctional patterns for love. Over time, I had to learn what love is, but also what it is not.

3. I NEEDED TO GET EQUIPPED IN WHO I REALLY AM.

Identity affirmation and validation is so important. Hearing that it's ok to have a sensitive heart was helpful, because it allowed me to stop looking at my sensitivities with disgust, but with love. Experiencing the Father's love equipped me to gain clarity on who I really am.

Don't apologize for being sensitive, just get that sensitivity grounded in the love and security that comes from Father God. Take time to learn how He made you and come into appreciation for the great qualities God designed you with.

AFFIRMING SENSITIVE HEARTS

I have called out a sensitive heart in many people, encouraging them to cultivate a life that harnesses that sensitivity for the Kingdom of God. King David was a great example of living with a sensitive heart. He was called a "man after God's own heart," pretty high-level title to be given.

His writings and experiences revealed his great sensitivities. He shared the ups and downs of life like no one else in the Bible. David was deeply in touch with the victories and wins in life, but was also able to access the heartache, pain and disappointments with great depth. He brought all those experiences to God and used them as incubators to process the life of his heart in a powerful way.

4. I RENOUNCED HYPERSENSITIVITY.

Being sensitive is totally ok. In fact, it's wonderful. But I didn't have to live hypersensitive, which caused me to become motivated by fear.

The enemy came against my sensitive heart to keep me trapped. I picked up on many thoughts that I did not even need to give attention to. But insecurity and double mindedness pulled me into the sidewinding thoughts of the adversary.

When you are hypersensitive, negative issues get heightened. Broken areas get inflamed. When I renounced hypersensitivity, over time, I saw my emotions becoming more stabilized. I could feel certain emotions, but they wouldn't pull me into the ditches like they did before. I felt more in control of my overall mood and emotional life.

I actually felt my health improve too. I don't guarantee this will happen for you, but I found that renouncing hypersensitivity helped my body to get more stabilized. In fact, allergies actually lessened; probably because my immune system was becoming less hypersensitive. My body was coming into alignment with how my thinking was changing.

5. ENGAGE WORK THAT MAKES ROOM FOR WHO YOU ARE.

In my younger years, I served as a youth pastor, while later on, moving into pastoring music and the arts. I also pastored a church for a number of years. Today I am a full-time writer, teacher and consultant on heart transformation. All these avenues have served in different ways for me to express my sensitive heart in a fulfilling way.

The more I am learning to appreciate who God made me to be, the easier it is for me to find my lane in making a difference. I recommend you find a way to use your sensitivity to bless others in the most fulfilling way. So, to get started, get into your own heart healing journey and share with others what you discover in a way that makes you come alive.

6. DEVELOP CLEAR AND LOVING BOUNDARIES.

Boundaries, boundaries, boundaries…

As someone who works with so many different people with very difficult battles, I have had to learn this, often the hard way. At first, I wanted to help everyone, but I've had to learn to establish proper boundaries, so that I could serve people in a healthy and more effective way.

With a sensitive heart, you need to learn what true love looks like and what healthy boundaries are. Get schooled in codependency and other toxic relationship patterns that can give you clarity on how to manage your heart better with others.

7. LEARN TO RELEASE ISSUES THAT ARE NOT YOURS.

I've had to get crystal clear on what is my burden to bear and what is not my responsibility. I discovered that a large percentage of what I carried was actually not mine to carry. Too many with sensitive hearts end up shouldering the burdens of others, to the detriment of their own hearts. But they do this in the name of love. Yet this is not always true love.

On top of it, they end up getting torn to shreds by the choices and sins of other people. I had to make a decision that I cannot want someone's freedom more than they do. I also cannot carry the sins and brokenness of people into my own inner life. This helped me to get clearer on what I am responsible for and drive out the clutter that stems from holding onto other people's bad choices.

8. DEVELOP A HEALTHY RHYTHM OF OUTPUT AND REFRESHMENT.

People that are sensitive often need more down time and refreshment than the average person. You can become more easily prone to burnout because of this. So, give yourself emotional margin. Make sure that you are getting into a good rhythm of pouring out with plenty of time to receive and recover. This is not a science, but an art. You have to learn what works for your life, makeup and structure.

Sensitive hearts experience the breadth and depth of life in powerful ways. But you don't have to live in that deep ocean 24/7. I spend my down time recovering in connection with God, but I also make a lot of room for simple things like walking, exercising, joking around, laughing and playing with family.

BE KIND TO YOURSELF

People with sensitive hearts that beat themselves up only make the journey harder. When you are having off days, take a step back and cut yourself a break. Give yourself time to realign and try again.

Learning to live with a sensitive heart is a gift; one that needs to be nurtured and honored. But no one taught us how to do this. So be kind and patient with yourself in the process.

QUESTIONS FOR CONSIDERATION:

1. Do you have a sensitive heart? Are there ways you looked down on your sensitivities?
2. Of the suggestions outlined in this chapter, which one would be the most helpful for you to keep in mind?
3. What would it look like for you to live powerfully from a sensitive heart?

PRAYER

Father God, I thank You for the heart that You have given me. I believe that You have given me a heart that is tender and sensitive towards You and was designed for a good purpose. I recognize that at times in my life, my heart has been hypersensitive in ways that were not helpful for my journey. I can even see where the enemy seeks to steal, kill and destroy the effectiveness that can come out of a sensitive heart.

So today, I come before You with my whole heart, asking that You take the sensitive areas of my heart and ground them in Your love. Heal the broken and empty places of my heart. Stabilize my heart with Your love, affection and validation. Show me who I am and help me to walk securely in that identity.

Grant me the wisdom and grace to know how to live from a healthy rhythm of life. I renounce any aspect of hypersensitivity, where fear has gotten a hold of my heart. I renounce fear and thoughts of apprehension that do not allow me to live powerfully from my heart.

Father, I thank You for how You made me. I make a decision to live confidently from the tender and sensitive heart You gave me. And I am grateful that You will walk with me through it all. In Jesus name I pray, amen.

27:
Finding Safe Relationships

Confess your trespasses to one another, and pray for one another, that you may be healed. James 5:16a

The subject of safe relationships can stir up conflict within our hearts. On one hand, we desire to experience powerful relationships. But on the other hand, most of our wounds and struggles stem from unsafe relationship experiences of the past.

Therefore, you are left with a decision to make, which will lead you down one of two pathways. One path is to withdraw from people and not bother ever getting close. Or you make the courageous decision to walk through healing and take steps to discover the potential found in safe relationship connection.

THE FOUNDATION OF EMOTIONAL HEALTH

I believe the foundation of all emotional health and sanity is found in the dimension of safe relationships. You and I need to learn to process relational safety on three levels: our relationship with God, ourselves and other people.

We learn to be safe with ourselves and God while in the midst of experiencing safe relationships with others. How we do life, connect and interact all contribute to the theme of healthy relationships.

You need various levels of relationships. There are acquaintances, friends, family and your community. Then there are those who make up your inner circle, the people that when you're going through something difficult or challenging, are those you can count on. You also have leaders, teachers and mentors who can be powerful influencers in your life.

Safe relationships are not relationships that are void of discomfort. All relationships need growth, maturing and seasons where you are stretched. Many run away when relationships get uncomfortable, right when they are on the verge of tremendous growth. Yet at the same time, there is a lot of damage that has been done, stemming from interactions with unsafe people.

THE NEED FOR QUALITY RELATIONSHIPS

For too long, culture has given much praise to talent, abilities and accomplishments, to the detriment of healthy relationships. It has cultivated a world of strong leaders who can accomplish great feats in public, but are miserable to be around privately. They can be full of unaddressed character issues and emotionally dangerous to be around.

I've met very impressive people and leaders who have become recognized names of influence, only to find that behind the scenes, there was very little relational depth and ability to genuinely connect.

Unfortunately, we have valued the outward, while ignoring the inward. We've worked on achievement while ignoring what's important. You can have impressive feats on your resume, but if you don't know how to do relationships well, you are living on a dead-end road.

Furthermore, Christians can value the vertical relationship with God, while dismissing and even avoiding the horizontal relationship with brothers and sisters. In fact, our relationship with each other is how we actually learn to grow in God the most. Most of the New Testament writing by the apostles tuned the believers towards how to do life with each other in healthy and powerful ways. James even said that our safe interactions can be a place of powerful confession and healing.

Confess your trespasses to one another, and pray for one another, that you may be healed. James 5:16a

There is tremendous healing power you can experience through the confession and sharing with other believers. But this must be in a safe context in order for that to even begin to take shape.

The problem is, too many gatherings are not safe anymore, or never were to begin with. But when safety is present, it becomes a treasured environment by which we can grow and heal to a greater potential. In order to manifest relationship safety, each of us has to work on our own issues, so that we can become safe. If you want safe relationships, you must first learn to be safe for others.

As you grow in the journey of becoming safe yourself, here are some questions you can ask to identify safe relationships:

1. DO THEY LIVE IN A "NO CONDEMNATION" ZONE?

The first sign of a safe relationship is that you can be flawed and vulnerable, yet still feel safe while connecting with this person. They cultivate what I call a "no condemnation zone" in how they interact with you.

You don't feel like you are being analyzed, judged or shamed. Your interactions with them never feel like an interrogation. (Trust me, I have been emotionally interrogated by people and it's the worst!)

If you share in a vulnerable way and get a condemning reaction of any kind, you will feel like reeling back in what you shared, rewinding and wishing you never brought up the subject. But when you interact with a safe person, they see your flaws and handle you with grace. I can literally feel the relief in my body as I write this, because that is what safe believers do. They allow you to be yourself, let your guard down and do life authentically.

Safe people carry a compassion that invites you to go deeper, knowing you are safe in those waters. We still have to face our fears, stemming from the hurts of the past and the shame we've experienced. But watching someone manifest a "no condemnation zone" sets the atmosphere for the relationship to flourish.

People who are religiously harsh, condemning and "judgy" don't get invited to people's homes. Trust me, I am not having them over for dinner. They won't get into my personal space, because they cannot handle it with grace. They will look for things to add to their rolodex of self-righteous and judgmental ammunition.

2. ARE THEY ALWAYS TRYING TO FIX YOU?

A safe person's number one priority is to experience loving connection with you. Their priority is not to fix you. If you find that someone's knee jerk reaction to your struggle is quick advice or the addition of a spiritual discipline, you may be interacting with an unsafe person.

Unfortunately, the "Christian Fixer" is in every church and community. They are uncomfortable with simply listening to what you are going through with empathy. In fact, they are often uncomfortable dealing with their own issues. So, they always respond to pain with a quick pad answer.

During some of the toughest seasons of my life, well-meaning people would react to what I was sharing with quick and shallow advice. Many times, I just needed someone to listen, to connect with me and hear me out. In fact, the power of just being heard can be way more healing than any advice someone can give.

Please understand something. I spend my life helping people. They call me to work on personal issues. And yet my number one goal in meeting with people is not to "fix" them. Priority one is that they feel safe in my presence. My prayer is that through our interactions, they can sense the love and grace of God in a meaningful way, where relationship safety can be restored.

If I can be a safe person, it gives room for God to work. It helps that person to be safe in their own thoughts and to take new steps towards freedom. I am never providing coaching until I sense there is safety in our interaction. When you show that kind of respect for another person's heart, it opens the door for maximum impact.

3. DO THEY KNOW HOW TO EMPATHIZE?

Safe people empathize. I believe one of the traits I want to teach my family and everyone I influence is how to empathize in relationships. Empathy involves the ability to understand and even feel what someone is going through.

Safe people can weep when you are suffering and will rejoice when you gain victory. They know how to experience the spectrum of emotions that you are going through and can connect to you in a way where you feel understood.

It is important to note that healthy empathizers are not pity party friends. They do not just take your pain and nosedive into the sea of despair every time you share a struggle. Safe people know how to first empathize so that you feel understood. They also have a way of using words and body language to make you feel encouraged and empowered, without demeaning your pain.

Safe people long for a breakthrough in your life, but in no way are they in a hurry to see you get fixed. This is because they know you are in process. When you leave the presence of a safe person who knows how to empathize, you gain a breath of fresh spiritual air, encouraged to go out there and face life with a new step.

4. HOW DO THEY TALK ABOUT THE STRUGGLES OF OTHERS?

There is a simple test off the jump to see if someone is safe. See how they respond to the struggle and mistakes of other people. This can be someone you both know or a famous name in the news headlines. Watch how they react to those situations and you will get a thermostat reading on how they will internally process your journey. If someone talks to you in a condemning way about others, there is a good chance they are doing that with what you are going through.

5. DO THEY KNOW HOW TO ACTIVELY LISTEN?

The art of listening is not a passive thing, but in fact a very active skill to practice. We live in an exhausting emotional world, where people are rushing to finish each other's sentences and move on, without doing any real listening.

Listening involves more than just nodding your head as someone talks. It means showing that you are paying attention to what they are saying and connecting to it.

Your response shows how well you listen more than anything else. If you respond to what others say by going into a story about yourself every time, then you are not really listening.

Active listeners hear the heart of what you are saying, because that's what they are looking for. They take time to understand what you're going through and feel a sense of your story and heart.

6. ARE THEY QUICK TO ASSUME?

Terrible listeners who are unsafe, show a pattern of interrupting conversations all the time. They often attempt to finish your sentences and communicate your thoughts for you. This comes out of many assumptions they may have about you.

Many people are quick to make assumptions in relationships, simply because it's a short cut. It gets to bottom line information fast, so your brain can categorize aspects of someone and move on to other things.

The problem is, many assumptions are wrong. The blanket statements that develop can create a very inaccurate picture that lacks compassion. Assumptions also dismiss the relational work of listening and empathizing. It actually shows a sign of being relationally lazy.

7. CAN THEY NAVIGATE UPS AND DOWNS WITH YOU?

This sign reveals if the relationship is going to be high maintenance or not. With an unsafe relationship, you have to put enormous energy into filtering your words, watching how you come across and hyper-analyzing what the other person might say. Basically, you can't be yourself.

Maybe for some relationships, you cannot have a bad day around this person. If you share something discouraging, they immediately try to snap you out of it and rush you into "feeling better." Other relationships are so toxic, they cannot handle you having victories or experiencing great breakthroughs. You can even feel an anger come off of them when you make some positive strides.

A safe person is not thrown into panic when you are going through a hard time. They are mature enough to know that we all go through challenging seasons and trials. They carry a groundedness, mainly because they have navigated through their own pain, which has prepared them to be safe for others.

8. ARE THEY TRUSTWORTHY WITH YOUR HEART?

A safe person honors and respects the vulnerable areas of your heart that are shared. When trust is compromised, safety is lost and the relationship can easily crumble. But when trust has been built with love and grace, the relationship has the potential to be a meaningful one for the long haul.

It is important that when someone allows you into the world of their heart, this invitation must be treated with kindness and respect. That is not the time to jump in, give know-it-all advice or ramble. This is the time to listen and earn someone's trust.

Most of our relationship battles have come down to trust being compromised in some way. Experience this enough and the easy temptation is to never trust again. But deep down, we all know that we cannot do life completely alone.

The good news is that God knows about all your trust issues. He is patient about them and willing to walk with you through the healing and recovery of where you have been hurt in relationships. In the long run, He desires to heal you and step by step, get you back into healthy connections.

WHERE DO I START?

The logical question many can ask here is, *"Where do I begin?"* If you want to experience safe relationships, start with being a safe person. Before you begin assessing the safety of those around you, begin by asking, *"Where can I learn to become a safe person in my relationships?"*

In the pursuit of safe relationships, don't buy into the expectation that you need to have crowds of safe people all around. If you have that, amazing. I am talking about having one, maybe two people in your life that you can process some of the vulnerable issues in life. Allow yourself time and prayerful consideration for how you can be safe and find those who can walk a safe, yet empowering journey with you.

QUESTIONS FOR CONSIDERATION:

1. In what ways have unsafe relationships of the past hindered your current ability to connect with new relationships?
2. In what ways can you learn to be a safer person in relationships?
3. Of the eight questions, which one helped you the most in finding safe relationships?
4. Which of the eight questions would be helpful for you to become safer for others?

PRAYER:

Father God, Your love reminds me that I am always safe with You. I thank You for Your covering, safety and protection, where I know I can take refuge in Your arms. I also recognize that my relationship with You is enhanced as I learn to interact with safe people.

As I learn to experience greater healing and transformation in my heart, I pray that You heal the areas of my heart that have been damaged by unsafe relationships. Father, help me to not hide in an emotional prison, but to take steps of faith towards new connections. Heal the wounds of my past. Help me to experience new references of relational safety.

I also ask that You help me to learn what it means to be a safe person with others. I make a commitment in my heart to be a trustworthy person, to demonstrate compassion and to be a safe vessel where others can experience the healing You are doing in their hearts. I pray this all in Jesus name, amen.

28:
Turning the Tables on Your Pain

...that we will be able to comfort those who are in any affliction with the comfort with which we ourselves are comforted by God.
2 Corinthians 1:3-4 (NASB)

During my time of pastoring, I had encouraged the church to get out there and help someone, primarily by using their own story as fuel to bless others. After the service, a woman walked up to me with a defeated look on her face.

She came under self-condemnation over the subject, because she felt that she had such a long way to go in her healing journey. She said to me, *"I don't feel like I can help anyone. It would be hypocritical, because I still have so much work to do in my own life."*

"And what's wrong with you helping others in the midst of that?" I asked.

"I would be a fraud, feeling like I'm performing. I have a long way to go myself, so I'd feel like an imposter."

My response was, *"It's not performance, fraud or living as an imposter if you simply be yourself and share out of what you have learned so far. When you express your authentic journey in that way, it's not performance. It is real life ministry."*

YOU GROW BY HELPING OTHERS

Helping others is not a replacement for dealing with your own issues. But helping others while you are allowing God to heal and transform your own heart can be incredibly powerful.

Heart healing takes practice. And I have found that one of the best ways I can empower the growth of my heart healing journey is by encouraging others and adding value to those God brings into my life. Quite often in my work, I can see my own battles in the person I am talking to. As I help them, I am reminding myself of what is true.

Blessed be the God and Father of our Lord Jesus Christ, the Father of mercies and God of all comfort, who comforts us in all our affliction so that we will be able to comfort those who are in any affliction with the comfort with which we ourselves are comforted by God.
2 Corinthians 1:3-4 (NASB)

It is simple. You feed others the spiritual food you have been eating and digesting. I am not talking about preaching to others or responding to their pain by having a teaching session. The first priority is to love on them and create an atmosphere of grace.

Then be yourself. Let the transformation that has taken place thus far manifest through your interactions. You are the message, so let who you are shine through.

TURNING THE TABLES ON THE ENEMY

The devil's mission is to steal, kill and destroy the life of your heart. In most cases, there was nothing you could have done to avoid those moments that hurt, broke or crushed you. But you can decide on what you'll do with it.

One of the greatest ways you can turn the tables on the enemy and the pain you have experienced is to help, encourage and empower others who are going through or who have been through similar battles that you have faced.

One of the greatest ways that people are impacted by my life is from the testimony of what I have been through and what I continue to grow in. My experience stems back to my journey as a pastor, who, through an emotional breakdown of anxiety, OCD, panic attacks and depression, began to seek God for help like never before. This positioned my heart to learn what I needed to know as I walked into freedom, while inviting others to engage the heart healing journey themselves.

God didn't cause these internal attacks, but He stepped into those places to teach me what I did not know. Without those painful rock bottom moments, I would have ignored the life of my heart and went on with life ignorantly, like many continue to do.

The awakening I experienced caused me to have a deep heart and compassion for the health of the church, which I have observed has been eroding for some time. We need heart surgery like never before. I have personally decided to be a part of the healing solution.

What I went through changed my trajectory completely. It opened a curtain to a "behind the scenes" view that I cannot "unsee." My heart is deeply moved to address the issues that are being neglected, overlooked and glossed over and are killing the life of the heart. I am deeply passionate that the church should be the greatest place for trauma, mental health, marriage struggles and addictions to be healed. I believe we should be manifesting the greatest relational fruit in our homes and families, not mirroring the same battles that an unredeemed world is showing.

Through some of my deepest battles, the enemy almost killed me. But since I chose to position my heart to learn, heal and awaken, God's faithfulness and love has been shed abroad in my heart. Like Neo from the movie *The Matrix*, I have seen a picture of the battle I cannot turn back from. I have been called to awaken, heal and transform hearts, one by one. What was sent to kill me has now become my ammunition every day.

HAVING REDEMPTIVE RADAR

When you allow God to heal and transform areas of your heart, it is a natural flow to have what I call "redemptive radar" for others. The word redeem means to "buy back." When God works powerfully in your heart, He brings back what was stolen. The redeeming work of Christ always involves restoring someone back to their original intended design.

What you've been through creates a sensitivity and compassion when you see it in others. If you've been effectively healed from addictions, then you have radar for those who are currently battling. You can almost detect them in a room without them saying anything. Your heart has a sensitivity for them.

Maybe you went through an abusive marriage that took every ounce of courage to get out of. You had to weed through years of healing self-hatred and guilt, while shedding off lies that God would not love you if you left. You went through excruciating decisions to walk free. Now you have redemptive radar for those who are in abusive marriages. They don't know what to do and suffer in silence, but your story can shed light on what is possible.

The same is true for mental health, marriage issues, parenting and every other battle we have faced in life. Whatever you have faced and sought to overcome, becomes an area that you have sensitivity towards. This can give you a highway to help others in a yielded flow of God's Holy Spirit. You are not speaking as an outsider, but as one who has been through the trenches.

Keep in mind that whatever you overcome in life, that area becomes real estate in which you have authority over. Because of what you have been through, you now carry an invitation for others to enter into the same breakthrough you have experienced. This is the mighty power of a living testimony. Even if you have made three steps of progress, those three steps are powerful gifts you can share with the rest of the body of Christ.

WHAT YOU WOULD HAVE THEM DO TO YOU

It's time that you bless others as a part of your healing journey. And there is a simple way you can do this. Do you remember the Scripture that is called the Golden Rule?

Therefore, whatever you want men to do to you, do also to them...
Matthew 7:12

In modern words, we know this command of Jesus as saying, *"Do to others what you would have them do to you."* So, what does this mean in your healing journey? Take a moment to think about what your greatest needs have been. Usually the answers to that question are connected to the wounds of your life.

For those of you that have been ignored, your greatest need was to be heard. For so long, that wound tormented your life and kept you from being at peace. But in the healing process, God is working that out with you.

So, if you want to do to others what you would want, the answer in this example is pretty simple. You would want people to listen to you, pay attention to you and notice you. So, do exactly that. Turn the tables on the enemy by giving out to others what you wish you could have received.

If you were disrespected, then show massive respect to everyone you see. If you were made fun of growing up or were embarrassed often, keep an eye out for those that may be going through the same thing and encourage them. If you were ignored a lot and left out, keep a radar out for those that seem to be ignored and give them your attention. By this you follow the Golden Rule and you turn the tables on the enemy with redemptive radar.

THE BLESSING OF THE HEART HEALING JOURNEY

As a result of entering into the heart healing journey, I have dedicated my life to helping others experience healing, freedom and transformation from the inside out. I get to help others with the very truth, healing and comfort I have received from God myself.

I have so much more to go, but I have experienced much healing already. My life will never be the same. How I see God, myself and others has radically changed, simply because I allowed God to have full access to my heart. I gave Him permission to show me through any means necessary, what my heart needed to walk in freedom.

The result has been a whole new way of thinking, believing and living. The biggest difference in my healing journey is that today I get to enjoy God, rather than run from Him, hide in fear of Him or tirelessly do things for Him with the hopes that He's pleased. I don't have to wander around in doubt, wondering if He notices me or even likes me. He's thrilled to know me and walk with me. I'm His creation and I'm destined to know Him.

I also get to enjoy every relationship that is in front of me. This begins with my wife and children, but spans out to the people I get to interact with. My life no longer has to be a consecutive non-stop chain of busy, pressure filled events. I have learned to enjoy the relationships God has put in my life, treasuring the moments, while allowing my heart to breathe in the love and grace that is available to me today.

What will be the message of your heart healing journey to others?

QUESTIONS FOR CONSIDERATION:

1. In what way can you begin sharing your heart healing journey with others?
2. If you were to title your heart healing journey, what would it be?

PRAYER:

Father God, I ask that You take everything I have been through in my journey and use it for Your glory. Thank You for bringing me this far. I know there is so much more ahead as You awaken, heal and transform my life more and more. Nothing I have experienced is wasted, especially as I allow You to heal, redeem and restore my life.

Today, I dedicate my journey to the work of encouraging and strengthening others. May every battle that I've gone through and every struggle I've faced and overcome be used to empower others. I pray that my life be a living testimony, so that others may be able to partake in what You have done in my own life.

Father, lead those down my path who can be encouraged and impacted by my story. Take everything that I have been through and use it to empower others. I make a decision to turn the tables on the enemy and use every place that has been challenging and turn it for Your glory. I thank You for all this. Here am I. Send me. In Jesus name I pray, amen.

markdejesus.com

Printed in Great Britain
by Amazon